Aeronautical Knowledge – Communications

Jeremy M Pratt

ISBN 9781906559823

Published by:
Airplan Flight Equipment Ltd

afeonline.com

This book is a guide to the CAA and EASA Communications Theoretical Knowledge syllabus for the Private Pilot Licence (PPL) and Light Aircraft Pilot Licence (LAPL) for aeroplanes.

This book is not intended to be an authoritative document and it does not in any way over-rule or counter instruction from an approved or registered training organisation or information or guidance produced by the Civil Aviation Authority (CAA), European Aviation Safety Agency (EASA) or by any other Competent Authority. Full reference should be made to applicable UK and EU regulations, Implementing Regulations and Acceptable Means of Compliance and Guidance Material (AMC/GM). Rules, procedures, limitations and guidance in documents produced by Competent Authorities, including but not limited to national law and guidance, Aeronautical Information Publications (AIP), Aeronautical Information Circulars (AIC) and the applicable Aircraft Flight Manual (AFM) – alternatively the Pilots Operating Handbook/Flight Manual (POH/FM) – must also be complied with at all times. Requirements of the aircraft operator, for example in an Operations Manual or flying order book, must also be complied with.

At the end of 2020 the UK formally left EASA; however for practical purposes EU and EASA regulations have been taken into UK law and there are few practical differences between UK and EASA aviation law. Where there are significant differences, these are noted in the 'National Procedures' section of this book. Aeronautical information, including that relating to Operational Procedures, can – and does – change frequently and it is the pilot's responsibility to remain up-to-date with such changes. The provisions of good airmanship and safe operating practice should be adhered to at all times.

Whilst every care has been taken in compiling this publication, relying where possible on authoritative and official information sources, the publisher and editorial team will not be liable in any way for any errors or omission whatsoever.

First edition 2018

Reprinted with amendments 2021

Copyright ©2018 & 2021
Airplan Flight Equipment Ltd
and Jeremy M Pratt

Aeronautical Knowledge – Communications

ISBN 9781906559823

Printed in Malta by Melita Press

Airplan Flight Equipment Ltd
1a Ringway Trading Estate,
Shadowmoss Road,
Manchester M22 5LH UK

www.afeonline.com

Contents

Intentionally Left Blank

Foreword and acknowledgements

This publication provides the Theoretical Knowledge (TK) required in Communications for non-commercial flight operations under Visual Flight Rules (VFR). It is based on the 2015 PPL and LAPL Theoretical Knowledge (TK) Operational Procedures syllabus published by the UK CAA and accepted by EASA and it is considered suitable for use in conjunction with training courses for the following pilot licences:

- EASA Private Pilot Licence (PPL) (Aeroplane)
- EASA Light Aircraft Pilot Licence (LAPL) (Aeroplane)
- CAA Private Pilot Licence (PPL) (Aeroplane)
- CAA Light Aircraft Pilot Licence (LAPL) (Aeroplane)
- UK National PPL (NPPL) (Aeroplane)
- ICAO-compliant PPL (Aeroplane) or equivalent licence
- Core knowledge for EASA and CAA Commercial Pilot Licence (CPL) (Aeroplane)
- Foundation knowledge for EASA and CAA Airline Transport Pilot Licence (ATPL) (Aeroplane)
- Foundation knowledge for EASA and CAA Multi-crew Pilot Licence (MPL) (Aeroplane)

This publication also provides foundation knowledge for an Air Transport Operations/ Management degree or similar academic qualification.

About the Author

Jeremy M Pratt took his first flying lesson at the age of 14, paid for by working in the hangar and radio unit at his local airfield. He gained his pilot's licence shortly after his 18th birthday after being awarded an Esso/Air League Flying Scholarship, became a flying instructor at 19 and a commercial pilot at the age of 20.

Since then he has taught (and continues to teach) pilots for a wide range of licences – both private and professional – as well as associated ratings and qualifications including night, instrument, tailwheel and multi-engine flying and he has flown General Aviation aircraft professionally in a number of other roles including pleasure flights, traffic reporting, aerial photography and aerial survey. He has owned and co-owned a number of General Aviation aircraft and flown a variety of aircraft types from Tiger Moth biplane to Cessna Citation jet, as well as trying-out helicopter, microlight and balloon flying. He also enjoys the highs (and occasional lows) of flying gliders.

The author's first flying training books were published in 1992, since when they have sold several hundred thousand copies world-wide and have been translated into a number of languages. He has also authored and co-authored around 25 additional aviation training books as well as contributing to various aviation publications including Flight Training News (FTN), for which he flight tests various aircraft types.

The author works with various aviation authorities and organisations on training and safety issues. He was also part of the team that produced the 2015 CAA/EASA PPL and LAPL syllabi and he sits on the CAA's PPL Theoretical Knowledge Working Group. He flies whenever he can find the time – for instructing, for business, for pleasure and for the sheer joy of flight.

Image Acknowledgements

Rights are reserved for all images used in this book. Where known the appropriate rights or copyright holder is listed below. If we have been unable to trace the rights holder for an image, it is marked 'ukn' (unknown). 'AFE' indicates Airplan Flight Equipment Ltd and/or Jeremy M Pratt.

C1 VHF Radio Broadcast

C1.1 © AFE; C1.2 © AFE; C1.3 © AFE; C1.4 © AFE

C2 Transmission Technique

C2.1 © AFE; C2.2 © AFE; C2.3 © AFE; C2.4 © AFE; C2.5 © AFE; C2.6 © AFE; C2.7 © AFE; C2.8 © AFE; C2.9 © AFE; C2.9a © Bendix King; C2.9b © Trig Avionics; C2.9c © Garmin; C2.10 © NASA; C2.11 © AFE; C2.12 © AFE; C2.13 © AFE; C2.14 © AFE; C2.15 © AFE; C2.16 © AFE

C3 VFR Communications Procedures

C3.1 © AFE; C3.2 © ASA; C3.3 © ICOM Ltd; C3.4 © AFE; C3.5 © AFE; C3.6 © AFE; C3.7 © AFE; C3.8 © AFE; C3.9 © AFE; C3.10 © AFE; C3.11 © AFE; C3.12 © AFE; C3.13 © AFE; C3.14 © Trig Avionics; C3.15 © AFE; C3.16 © AFE; C3.17 © AFE; C3.18 © AFE; C3.19 © AFE; C3.20 © AFE; C3.21 © AFE

C4 Weather Information

C4.1 courtesy AIP; C4.2 courtesy AIP

C5 Communications Failure

C5.1 © AFE; C5.2 © AFE; C5.3 © AFE; C5.4 © AFE; C5.5 © AFE;

C6 Distress and Urgency Procedures

C7 National Procedures

C7.0 courtesy AIP; C7.1 © AFE; C7.2 © AFE; C7.3 © AFE; C7.4 © AFE; C7.5 © UK VFR Flight Guide; C7.6 © AFE; C7.6a © UK VFR Flight Guide; C7.7 © AFE; C7.8 © AFE; C7.9 © AFE; C7.9a © AFE; C7.10 courtesy AIP; C7.10a courtesy CAA/NATS; C7.10b courtesy AIP; C7.11 © AFE; C7.12 © AFE; C7.13 © AFE; C7.14 courtesy AIP; C7.15 courtesy AIP; C7.16 © AFE; C7.17 © AFE; C7.18 courtesy CAA/NATS; C7.19 courtesy AIP; C7.20 courtesy AIP; C7.21 Crown Copyright; C7.22 courtesy Edinburgh Airport; C7.23 courtesy CAA

Acknowledgements

Creating a book is, rather like flying itself, an activity that needs the help and assistance of a whole range of people to bring the dream into reality. I have been fortunate over the years to have met, flown and worked with a range of very talented people in both the aviation and publishing worlds and many of them have, in one way or another, contributed to this book. The following are just some of the people and organisations who have directly contributed or worked on this book, and I offer my heartfelt thanks to them. To any person or organisation I may have inadvertently missed out, I additionally offer my apologies for the oversight.

Airplan Flight Equipment (AFE)

Wendy Barratt

Civil Aviation Authority

Crécy Publishing

Eurocontrol

Flight Training News

Brighton City Airport

Rob Taylor – GDi studio

National Air Traffic Services

Dave Unwin

And, of course, my long-suffering family who continue to put-up with my business trips away, late evenings in the office, flying weekends and working weekends for reasons I've never fully understood.

I know that you think you heard what you thought I said;
however;
I don't think you realise that what I said is not what you
thought you heard.

(RAF flight safety poster circa 1973).

Introduction

It's not an uncommon scenario. During an early flying lesson, the student pilot goes through the starting procedures and is ready to taxi. At this point the instructor presses a small button hidden somewhere in the cockpit and transmits something to the effect of:

"Golf Michaelangelo whispering klingons, situation over bar the frying pan apron, free quest hair field de partsure in formation hand taxy destruction. Over."

While the student is still trying to get a grip on the meaning of this, a stream of similar nonsense materialises out of the ether and into the student's headset. This obviously has some significance to the instructor, because she/he nods meaningfully and makes some notes on a pad. Then some form of reply goes back:

"Roger's got that. Queue and ache ones hero two trees, quiffy ones hero one time, taxy two runaway in puce zero height, golf whisk-key key low."

This procedure is repeated at regular intervals throughout the flight, while the student thinks something along the lines of 'The flying is straight-forward enough, but this radio business is going to take some really hard work'. The student is even more bemused when the instructor insists that the internationally recognised language for aviation radio communications is English…

In fact, the basics of radio phrases and procedures are easy enough once you understand some of the standard phrases and conventions used. It's not unlike learning the basics of another language; once you can use a simple phrase (*"I'd like a coffee please"*) and can anticipate the sort of reply you are likely to receive (*"Certainly, that will be three euros"*) a lot of the fear goes out of the process.

The emphasis on the use of standard words and phrases, and conventions for how pilots and controllers talk to each other, are essential elements in safe aviation communications. Even where the pilot and controller share the same mother language, the potential for confusion or misunderstanding is magnified once non-standard phraseology is used. The potential for mix-ups becomes even more likely if those involved in the conversation have different native languages, even if they both understand 'aviation' English. You will also find that many of the phrases and conventions of aviation radio communications are used in everyday aviation conversations too.

This publication concentrates on radio telephony (RTF) procedures applicable to the VFR pilot eg a student pilot or a pilot without instrument qualifications. For this reason, phraseology and procedures relating specifically to Instrument Flight Rules – IFR – operations (flight in airways, instrument approaches etc.) are not covered here. Bear in mind also that radio communications procedures and phrases do change over time, so it is necessary to keep up-to-date with current usage.

In any event, although you may feel that you have more than enough to do in the early stages of learning to fly, without having to talk to people on the ground at the same time, the fact is that the sooner you begin to use the radio and understand the basic phrases and conventions, the quicker you will feel confident, and become competent, in radio communications. If you have an air-band radio, listening to everyday conversation on aviation frequencies is very useful and to some extent can save you the pressure of trying to learn radio procedures and learn to fly the aircraft simultaneously.

A final point. Once you know the standard communications phrases and procedures, it pays to stick to them. Few things are more frustrating to pilots and controllers alike than a 'Walter Mitty' character who monopolises a radio frequency with long monologues about their flight, their life in general and their favourite non-standard phraseology. We've all heard them, and you will too. Most pilots prefer to treat the radio as an aid to the safety of their flight, not an excuse to hear their own voice, and those sharing the frequency and the skies with them are grateful for that.

After all, wouldn't you prefer to be flying an aircraft rather than just talking about it?

Jeremy M Pratt
April 2018

Intentionally Left Blank

VHF Radio Broadcast

Factors affecting VHF radio range

Progress check

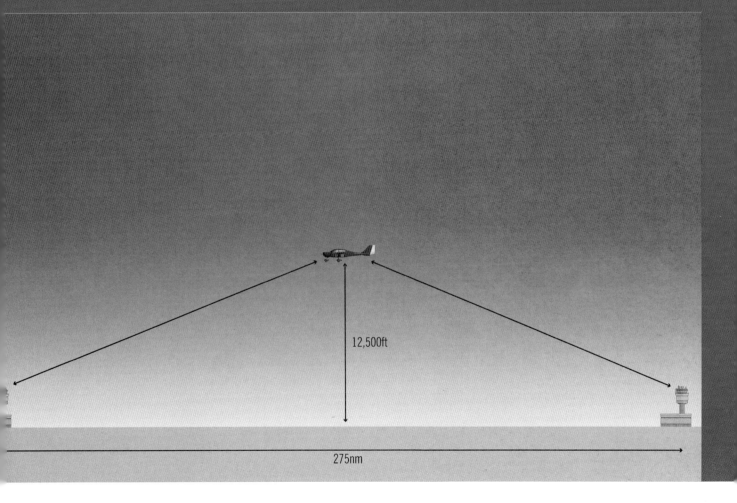

12,500ft

275nm

VHF Radio Broadcast

C1

Factors affecting VHF radio range

Virtually all voice communications between General Aviation (GA) aircraft and ground stations take place via radio transmissions in the **Very High Frequency** (**VHF**) band, which covers the frequency range from 30 megahertz (MHz) to 300MHz. The VHF band is also used by services including FM commercial radio, marine radio, emergency communications and some radio navigation aids. Within the VHF band, civilian aircraft voice communications (sometimes called 'radiotelephony' or 'rtf') take place in the frequency range between **118MHz and 137MHz**.

Name	Designator	Frequency Range	Usage
Very Low Frequency	**VLF**	3kHz – 30kHz	Omega long range navigation aid
Low Frequency	**LF**	30kHz – 300kHz	Aviation and maritime navigation aids
Medium Frequency	**MF**	300kHz – 3MHz	Aviation and maritime navigation aids, AM commercial radio broadcast
High Frequency	**HF**	3MHz – 30MHz	Long range maritime and aviation communication, 'short wave' commercial radio
Very High Frequency	**VHF**	30MHz – 300MHz	Maritime and aviation communications, FM commercial radio, TV broadcast, emergency services radio
Ultra High Frequency	**UHF**	300MHz – 3GHz	Military aircraft communications, aircraft radar, TV broadcast, mobile phone,
Super High Frequency	**SHF**	3GHz – 300GHz	Radio astronomy, radar and satellite

Figure C1.1
Radio frequency bands.

It is a feature of VHF radio that the electromagnetic waves that make up a VHF radio transmission and travel at around the speed of light, also travel in a straight line. This feature of VHF transmissions is often described as **line-of-sight** – in other words if you could theoretically see a point in perfect visibility, a VHF transmission from you should reach it. If a point is beyond line of sight (for example, over the earth's horizon), or blocked by some other solid object (such as a mountain), a VHF transmission will probably not reach it.

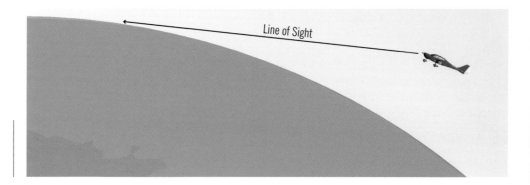

Figure C1.2
VHF radio transmissions travel mostly in a straight line and so VHF range is dictated by the 'line-of-sight' principle.

As height above the surface increases, so the line-of-sight distance to the horizon increases and the range of a VHF transmission to or from a surface point also increases. On the ground, the distance to the horizon is around 2.5 nautical miles, so that is the theoretical range of a VHF radio transmission to a point on the ground (although in practice, a VHF radio transmission travels slightly beyond the horizon). If a VHF radio is now taken to 1000 feet above the surface, its transmissions can reach to a point on the surface around 39 nautical miles away. Increase height to 10,000 feet and VHF range to the surface becomes approximately 122 nautical miles.

Increasing the height of a VHF radio installation increases its range, which is why ground-based radio antennas are placed on top of masts on high ground or high buildings. As aircraft fly higher the range of their VHF transmission also increases and their transmissions can be heard by pilots on other airborne aircraft at a greater range than by operators of ground-based radios.

For practical purposes, the quality and range of VHF radio transmissions are not altered by weather factors (such as rain, fog, thunderstorms etc.), nor by time of day.

Height	Theoretical VHF range
1000ft	39nm
3000ft	67nm
5000ft	86nm
10,000	122nm
13,000	140nm

Figure C1.3
Increase in theoretical VHF range as height above the surface increases.

Nevertheless, there are some unusual atmospheric conditions which can greatly increase the range of VHF transmissions – although they do so in an unpredictable way.

A temperature inversion in the lower atmosphere (where temperature increases with increasing height, the opposite of the normal situation) can lead to a phenomena known as **duct propagation**. When this occurs, the range of VHF transmissions at low levels may increase by two or three times their normal distance and aircraft may unexpectedly hear transmissions to or from an airfield hundreds of miles away.

Even more rarely, unusual activity in the ionosphere (part of the upper atmosphere) called **sporadic E** can massively increase the range of VHF transmissions.

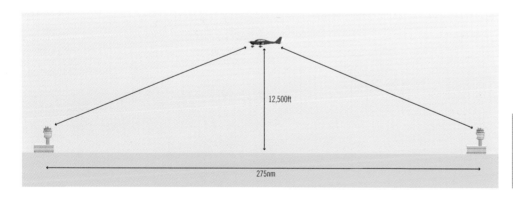

12,500ft

275nm

Figure C1.4
Theoretically, an aircraft flying at 12,500ft or above halfway between Gloucestershire and Dundee could speak to both towers simultaneously on the same frequency.

Because there are a limited number of radio frequency channels available in the VHF band, it is not possible to allocate a frequency to one station only and the same frequency will be used by different ground stations and facilities. Planners will try to ensure that airfields or services using the same frequency are as far apart as possible, to avoid interference. Even so, radio transmissions from a high-flying aircraft may be capable of reaching an unintended airfield or service if a pilot attempts to make contact at an extreme range. For example, within the British Isles, Gloucestershire airport tower and Dundee airport tower use the same VHF frequency. The two ground stations are around 275 nautical miles apart, so an aircraft flying halfway between the two at 12,500 feet will, in theory at least, be able to communicate with both control towers on the same frequency.

Out of interest, long-distance aircraft voice communications (for example over the oceans) is achieved via High Frequency (HF) radio, which has much greater range than VHF radio, but is affected by factors such as time of day, seasons and sun activity.

Progress check

1. Within which frequency band do most General Aviation voice communications take place?
2. What is the range-limiting feature of VHF transmissions?
3. In general, as an aircraft flies higher what is the effect on the range of its radio transmissions?
4. In what circumstances might VHF transmissions have a much greater range than expected?

These questions are intended to test knowledge and reinforce some of the key learning points from this section. In answering these questions, a 'pass rate' of about 80% should be the target.

Model answers are found at page C93

C2

Transmission Technique

Transmission of letters

Transmission of numbers

Transmission of time

Call signs

Progress check

Transmission Technique

Transmission of letters

The international standard is that the English language is used in aviation voice communications, (although local languages are also widely used, especially at non-international airfields). To minimise confusion, particularly in radio communications, in the 1950s the International Civil Aviation Organisation (ICAO) adopted a system called the **phonetic alphabet**, in which each letter of the English alphabet is allocated a specific phonetic word with a specified pronunciation. The appropriate code word and pronunciation is used whenever an individual letter needs to be transmitted (for example an aircraft registration, a taxiway or holding point designator, a radionavigation aid or route designator).

In the table below the fragment of the phonetic word in bold italics is the part of the word to be emphasised:

Letter	Phonetic Word	Pronunciation	Letter	Phonetic Word	Pronunciation
A	Alpha	*AL* FAH	N	November	NO *VEM* BER
B	Bravo	*BRAH* VOH	O	Oscar	*OSS* CAH
C	Charlie	*CHAR* LEE	P	Papa	PAH *PAH*
D	Delta	*DELL* TAH	Q	Quebec	KEH *BECK*
E	Echo	*ECK* OH	R	Romeo	*ROW* ME OH
F	Foxtrot	*FOKS* TROT	S	Sierra	SEE *AIR* RAH
G	Golf	GOLF	T	Tango	*TANG* GO
H	Hotel	HO *TELL*	U	Uniform	*YOU* NEE FORM
I	India	*IN* DEE AH	V	Victor	*VIK* TAH
J	Juliett	*JEW* LEE *ETT*	W	Whiskey	*WISS* KEY
K	Kilo	*KEY* LOH	X	X-ray	*ECKS* RAY
L	Lima	*LEE* MAH	Y	Yankee	*YANG* KEY
M	Mike	MIKE	Z	Zulu	*ZOO* LOO

Figure C2.1
The Phonetic alphabet

The phonetic alphabet is used extensively in aviation, not just during radio communications but also in telephone conversation and even face-to-face dialogue. Indeed, its use is so common that many pilots use phonetic letters in normal conversation without realising it (and some do it just to try to impress!).

It helps to become comfortable with the phonetic alphabet as quickly as possible, so that it's one less element that has to be consciously translated in the initially unfamiliar language of aviation communications. A good way to learn the phonetic alphabet is to make a point of converting groups of letters you see in everyday life – car registration or licence plates, addresses, abbreviations etc. into their correct phonetic words and pronunciations. Very soon the phonetic alphabet will become second nature.

Transmission of numbers

As with the phonetic alphabet, in aviation communications numbers are given specific pronunciations in order to avoid confusion between digits that can sound familiar:

Number	Spoken word	Pronunciation	Number	Spoken word	Pronunciation
0	zero	*ZE-RO*	7	seven	*SEV*-en
1	one	*WUN*	8	eight	*AIT*
2	two	*TOO*	9	nine	*NIN*-er
3	three	*TREE*	10	ten	*TEN*
4	four	*FOW*-er	11	eleven	*EE-LEV-EN*
5	five	*FIFE*	12	twelve	*TWELF*
6	six	*SIX*			

Figure C2.2
The pronunciation of numbers.

These pronunciations are easily learnt by converting numbers that you come across in every-day life into their correct pronunciation.

The 'default' protocol in aeronautical communications is that each digit of a number is transmitted individually. So, for example, runway 11 is referred to as "*runway one one*", not "*runway eleven*". Indeed, the European Standardised Rules of the Air (SERA) require that: "*all numbers used in the transmission of aircraft call sign, headings, runway, wind direction and speed shall be transmitted by pronouncing each digit separately*."

Here are some examples of transmitting numbers in aviation communications by speaking each digit of a number separately.

Type of number	Example	Transmitted as
Aircraft Call Sign	Mersey 628	Mersey six two eight
Flight Level	Flight level 120	Flight level one two zero
Direction	345°	three four five
Transponder code	4732	four seven three two
Runway	19	one nine
Altimeter setting	1026	one zero two six

Figure C2.3
Examples of transmission of numbers.

From here on the phonetic pronunciation of letters and numbers is omitted from sample radio transmissions for clarity, the reader should convert each letter and number into the correct phonetic pronunciation for good practice.

In addition to individual digits, other spoken numerals also have defined pronunciations:

Numeral	Pronunciation
Hundred	*HUN*-dred
Thousand	*TOU-SAND*
Decimal	*DAY-SEE-MAL*

Figure C2.4
Other numerical pronunciations.

In a small number of specific instances, the terms 'hundred' and 'thousand' are used to avoid the time-consuming repetition of zeros (pronunciation is omitted from here for clarity):

Type of number	Example	Transmitted as
Aircraft altitude or height	900	nine hundred
	3400	three thousand four hundred
Cloud altitude or height	700	seven hundred
	8000	eight thousand
Visibility	500	five hundred
	1200	one thousand two hundred
A pressure setting of 1000hPA	1000hPa	one thousand
Flight levels of whole hundreds	FL200	Flight Level two hundred
A transponder code of whole thousands	7000	seven thousand

Figure C2.5
Use of 'hundred' and 'thousand' in radio transmissions.

Although there are regional variations, generally the following units of measurement are common in aviation communications through Europe and in most parts of the world, and so are often omitted from verbal messages:

Measurement	term omitted
Airspeed and wind speed	Knots (one knot equals one nautical mile per hour)
Distance in navigation	nautical miles
Direction	Degrees magnetic
Visibility (up to 5000 metres)	Metres
Visibility (above 5 kilometres)	Kilometres
Vertical distance	feet
Vertical speed	feet per minute
Altimeter setting	Hectopascals
Air Temperature	degrees Celsius

Figure C2.6
Standard aviation units of measurement.

Aviation radio frequencies are defined as '**megahertz**' (**MHz**) and fractions of MHz – '**kilohertz**' (**kHz**). When written down, selected on a radio or spoken, MHz and kHz are separated by a decimal point.

Until the early part of this century, aviation radio frequencies were allocated to two decimal places, with a spacing between frequencies of 25kHz. Therefore, a radio frequency consisted of five digits:

Radio Frequency	Transmitted as
118.65	*"One one eight **decimal** six five"*
124.05	*"One two four **decimal** zero five"*
134.75	*"One three four **decimal** seven five"*

Figure C2.7
25kHz radio frequencies.

Where the last digit is a zero, it can be omitted:

Radio Frequency	Transmitted as
122.30	*"One two two **decimal** three"*
129.00	*"One two nine **decimal** zero"*

Figure C2.8
Omitting zeros from radio frequencies.

As the aviation radio frequency band has become more congested, many states – including many of those in Europe – are now defining radio frequencies (sometimes called 'channels') to three decimal places, so that a radio frequency (or channel) consists of six digits in 8.33kHz steps. In general, all six digits are transmitted, except where both the fifth and sixth digits are both zero:

Radio Frequency	Transmitted as
127.675	*"One two three **decimal** six seven five"*
119.025	*"One one nine **decimal** zero two five"*
133.100	*"One three three **decimal** one"*
124.780	*"One two four decimal seven eight zero"*

Figure C2.9
8.33kHz radio frequencies.

Figure C2.9a, Figure C2.9b, Figure C2.9c
Some typical aircraft radios showing different methods of presenting the communication frequency in use, as well as any 'standby' or 'monitoring' frequency.

Transmission of time

Within aviation, time is usually referred to in terms of **Universal Coordinated Time** (**UTC**), which in practical terms is the successor to GMT (Greenwich Mean Time). UTC does not vary by location or season – when it is 11:00 UTC in London, it is also 11:00 UTC all over the world (and off it – the International Space Station uses UTC).

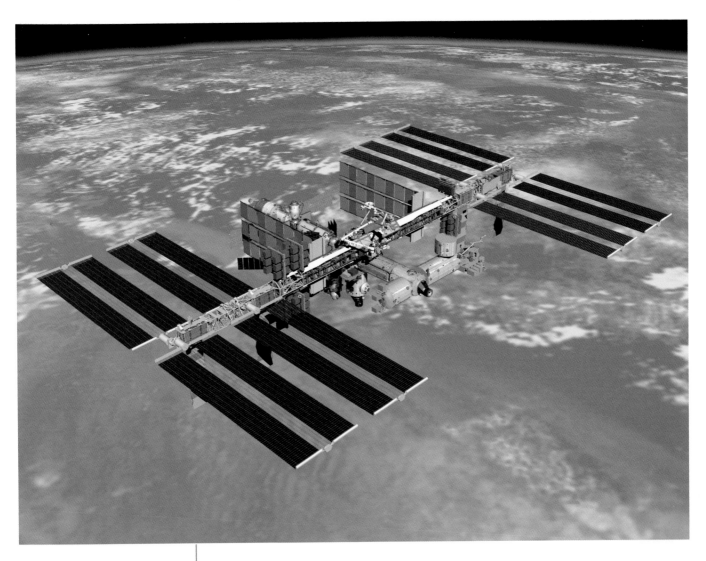

Figure C2.10
The International Space Station uses UTC as its
time reference.

The world is divided into 24 principle time zones, each of which is 'off-set' by a certain number of whole hours (either plus or minus) from UTC (there are also a number of additional time zones with 30 or 45 minutes 'off-sets'). Within the '0' time zone there is zero off-set from UTC, which is why UTC is sometimes referred to as '**Z**' or '**Zulu**' time.

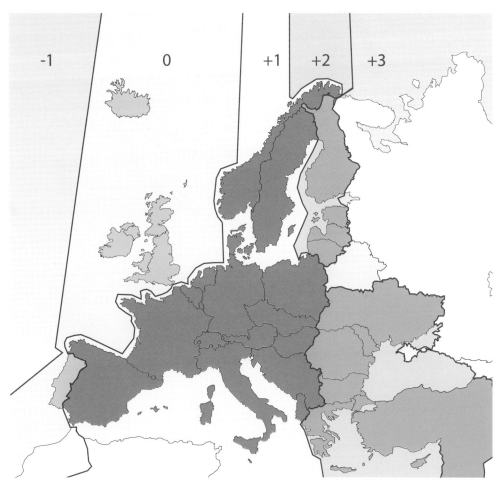

Figure C2.11
European time zones.

Figure C2.12
A '24 hour' clock face.

Figure C2.13
It is quite common in the aviation world to see clocks marked as 'Z' or 'Zulu', indicating that they are displaying UTC.

Within aviation, time is referred to using the 24 hour clock to avoid confusion between morning and afternoon times:

12 hour clock	24 hour clock	12 hour clock	24 hour clock
12:00 (midnight)	00:00 (start of day)	12:00 (noon)	12:00
1:00 am	01:00	1:00 pm	13:00
2:00 am	02:00	2:00 pm	14:00
3:00 am	03:00	3:00 pm	15:00
4:00 am	04:00	4:00 pm	16:00
5:00 am	05:00	5:00 pm	17:00
6:00 am	06:00	6:00 pm	18:00
7:00 am	07:00	7:00 pm	19:00
8:00 am	08:00	8:00 pm	20:00
9:00 am	09:00	9:00 pm	21:00
10:00 am	10:00	10:00 pm	22:00
11:00 am	11:00	11:00 pm	23:00
		12:00 pm (midnight)	24:00 (end of day)

Figure C2.14
The 24 hour clock.

When time is transmitted in aviation communications, and where no confusion will take place, only minutes past the hour are used, with each digit transmitted separately. So an airborne time of 13:43 might be transmitted as "*Airborne at four three*".

Call signs

An aircraft will normally be allocated a **call sign** before flight and it must not change that call sign during the flight, unless instructed to do so by an Air Traffic Controller.

In 'General Aviation' (GA) operations, the most common call sign is simply the aircraft's registration using the phonetic alphabet, eg an aircraft with the registration D-HATC may use the radio call sign "*Delta Hotel Alpha Tango Charlie*".

Occasionally the pilot or operator may choose to include the aircraft model or manufacturer in the call sign, eg a Cessna with the registration F-EMGP becomes "*Cessna Foxtrot Echo Mike Golf Papa*".

If the aircraft operator has been allocated a designator by an aviation authority, this designator may be used together with the last four characters of the aircraft's registration, for example "Slickair Bravo Lima India Kilo".

More commonly, if the operator has an allocated radio designator, the call sign will be that designator followed by a numerical flight identification, eg "*Heronair 486*"

When an aircraft first makes contact on a radio frequency, the full call sign must be used, and the call sign can only be abbreviated if the ground station (not the aircraft) abbreviates it first. Where a call sign is permitted to be abbreviated, the abbreviation is done in accordance with the following convention (the phonetic code words are omitted here for clarity):

Call Sign Type	Permitted abbreviation	Example
Aircraft registration	first and last two characters of the registration	G-ABCD becomes 'G-CD'
Aircraft manufacturer or model plus registration	Manufacturer or model plus last two characters of the registration	Tecnam I-EYNO becomes 'Tecnam NO'
Operator designation plus registration	Operator designation plus the last two characters of the registration	Modernair HB-ZPR becomes 'Modernair PR'
Operator designation plus flight identification	No abbreviation permitted	Sparkair 853 – must be used in full at all times

Figure C2.15
Abbreviation of Call Signs.

Ground stations are also allocated call signs, which normally consist of a unit location (for example an airfield) and a suffix which indicates the type of service being given.

Air traffic control units offer a 'control' service, the nature of which is indicated by a specific call sign suffix:

ATC service	Call Sign Suffix	Example
Area Control Service	**Control**	London Control
Radar	**Radar**	Cardiff Radar
Approach Control	**Approach**	Newcastle Approach
Aerodrome Control	**Tower**	Newquay Tower
Surface Movement Control	**Ground**	Gatwick Ground

Figure C2.16
Air Traffic Control call signs.

Only an Air Traffic Control unit can offer an ATC clearance or instruction. An **ATC clearance** is authorisation for an aircraft to proceed under the conditions specified. An **ATC instruction** is a directive issued by ATC requiring a pilot to take a specific action.

A **Flight Information Service** is a service provided to give advice and information useful for the safe and efficient conduct of flights. A Flight Information Service (FIS) must provide flights with urgent en-route meteorological information; important changes in aeronautical information (for example short notice airfield closures); airfield meteorological information; and information on 'collision hazards' for aircraft operating in class C, D, E, F and G airspace. In practice, a flight information service can only advise in relation to traffic it is aware of, and outside controlled airspace (ie Classes F and G) there may well be a very high percentage of airborne traffic which is not known to any single FIS unit. Where a flight information service is provided to a VFR flight, it will provide, as far as possible, any information about traffic or weather conditions along the route of the flight which are likely to make VFR flight impracticable. The fact that a flight is receiving a Flight Information Service does not relieve the pilot-in-command of any responsibilities at all and the pilot-in-command must make the final decision on any suggested alteration of flight plan.

A Flight Information Service can be either provided for a region (such as a Flight Information Region – FIR) or a specific airfield, and uses the call sign suffix 'Information', for example:

Scottish Information
Goodwood Information

Where a Flight Information Service (FIS) is provided at a specific airfield, it is known as an **Aerodrome Flight Information Service** (**AFIS**) and it provides information for traffic at the airfield and in the vicinity of the airfield.

An aeronautical station not offering an ATC or flight information service may use the call sign suffix 'radio', for example:

Skerries Radio

Within this book, the term 'Air Traffic Service Unit' ('ATSU') is used to describe any unit offering an ATC, flight information or 'radio' service.

The full call sign of an ATSU should always be used when first establishing communications, and if a pilot uses the wrong call sign, the ATSU will normally be quick to state the proper call sign. Once good two-way communication has been established, and there is no risk of confusion, it may be permissible to omit the location name or the suffix of the ATSU.

The correct radio call sign for an ATSU (or 'Aeronautical Station' as ICAO calls it) will be found in the appropriate **Aeronautical Information Publication** (**AIP**), together with the appropriate frequency, hours of operation etc. Details for communications services at airfields will be found in the 'Aerodrome' (AD) section. Details for en-route communications services are found, logically enough, in the 'En-route' (ENR) section of the AIP.

The entire network of aeronautical ground stations and aircraft with radios involved in RTF communications is collectively known to ICAO, and other aviation authorities, as the 'aeronautical mobile service'.

Progress check

5.   What is the correct phonetic word and pronunciation for the letter R?

6.   What is the correct phonetic pronunciation for the number four?

7.   What is the 'default' situation when transmitted a multi-digit number?

8.   Give one example of a number where the terms 'hundred' and/or 'thousand' can be used in aviation communications.

9.   How should a radio frequency of 120.405 be transmitted (phonetic pronunciation not required)?

10.   How should a radio frequency of 135.700 be transmitted?

11.   Using the 24 hour clock, describe a time of 3:30 in the afternoon.

12.   Where an ATSU permits it, what is the correct abbreviation of the call sign G-PEWR?

13.   How can an ATC clearance be defined?

14.   What is a Flight Information Service?

15.   What sort of ATSU may use the call sign 'Radio'?

16.   Where will details of an ATSU's services, call sign, operating hours and frequency be found?

These questions are intended to test knowledge and reinforce some of the key learning points from this section. In answering these questions, a 'pass rate' of about 80% should be the target.

Model answers are found at page C93

Intentionally Left Blank

C3

VFR Communications Procedures

Test procedures

Standard phraseology

Items requiring read back

Transfer of communications

Transponder operating procedures

Progress check

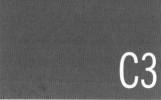
VFR Communications Procedures

Test procedures

To check if radio transmissions are being received properly, a **test transmission** can be made. When this procedure is used (it's not obligatory), it is usually the first radio call on that frequency from the aircraft and should take the following form:

1. The identification (ie the call sign) of the aeronautical station being called;
2. The aircraft identification (normally its call sign);
3. The words "Radio Check";
4. The frequency being used.

For example, a request for a radio check from an aircraft with the registration EI-NFW, on the ground at Cork airport, would sound like this:

"Cork Ground, India Echo November Foxtrot Whiskey, radio check, 121 decimal 85"

The reply also has an established format:

1. The identification (call sign) of the aircraft calling
2. The identification (call sign) of the station responding;
3. The 'readability' of the transmission.

Radio transmissions can be classified in terms of their **readability** using the following scale:

Readability scale	Description
1	Unreadable
2	Readable now and then
3	Readable but with difficulty
4	Readable
5	Perfectly readable

Figure C3.1
The readability scale of radio transmissions.

Figure C3.2
In most General Aviation aircraft, the use of a headset is highly recommended.

Figure C3.3
In some aircraft, a fixed speaker and handheld microphone may be used for radiotelephony communications.

So, the reply to the example request for radio check shown above, might be:

"*India Echo November Foxtrot Whiskey, Cork Ground, Readability 4*"

The replying station might choose to add additional information about the aircraft's radio transmission, for example:

"*India Echo November Foxtrot Whiskey, Cork Ground, Readability 3 with a loud background whistle*"

Or, if you are not having a good day:

"*Station calling Cork Ground, Readability 1*"

It worth remembering that unlike a telephone conversation, in aeronautical radio communications only one person can speak at a time – if two stations transmit simultaneously on the same frequency, the result is likely to be a loud 'squeal' heard by everyone else on frequency, or just a jumble of words over the top of each other.

There are some points of good **transmitting technique** which help radio transmissions to be heard and understood as clearly as possible. The following list is based on advice from ICAO and the UK Civil Aviation Authority:

1. Listen out before transmitting to make sure you are not interrupting an ongoing exchange. Check that the radio volume is set at the optimum level.

2. Do not turn your head away from the microphone whilst talking or vary the distance between it and your mouth while speaking – this is not normally a problem when using a headset. Severe distortion of speech may arise from:

    * talking too close to the microphone;

    * touching the microphone with the lips; or

    * holding the microphone or boom of a headset.

3. Use a normal conversation tone, speak clearly and distinctly.

4. Maintain an even rate of speech not exceeding 100 words per minute. If you know that elements of the message will have to be written down by the recipient, speak at a slightly slower rate.

5. Maintain the speaking volume at a constant level.

6. A slight pause before and after numbers will make them easier to understand.

7. Plan what you are going to say before starting to transmit, avoid hesitation sounds such as "*er*".

8. Avoid excessive use of courtesies and entering into non-operational conversations.

9. Depress the transmit switch fully before speaking and do not release it until the message is complete.

10. The mother tongue of the person receiving the message may not be English. Therefore, speak clearly and in any event use standard radiotelephony words and phrases wherever possible.

There is an established order of priority for different categories of radio message – not all conversations are equal! The order of precedence is applied so that the most urgent radio conversations will not be interrupted by more routine messages.

Priority	Message Category	Notes
1	Distress calls and messages	May be prefixed with the word 'Mayday'
2	Urgency call and messages	May be prefixed with the words 'Pan Pan'
3	Communications related to direction finding	
4	Flight safety messages	includes: – movement and control messages – messages of immediate concern to an aircraft in flight – meteorological information of immediate concern to an aircraft – messages concerning aircraft in flight or about to depart
5	Meteorological messages	
6	Flight regularity messages	

Figure C3.4
The order of precedence of aviation radio communication.

Standard phraseology

To avoid confusion or ambiguity in aeronautical communications, there is a relatively short list of standardised words and phrases which are recognised internationally and each of which has a very precise meaning. It is important to know this phraseology, to understand exactly what each word or phrase means and not to lapse into non-standard words or phrases. Under the Standardised Rules of the Air (SERA), **standard phraseology** must be used in all situations where it is specified, with plain language only used when standard phraseology cannot be used for the intended transmission.

The following table of standard words and phrases is set-out for reference, but by far the best way to learn them is by putting them into practice.

Figure C3.5
Some standard phraseology for aviation radio communications.

Word/Phrase	Meaning	Notes
ACKNOWLEDGE	Let me know that you have received and understood this message	
AFFIRM	Yes	
APPROVED	Permission for the proposed action is granted	
BREAK	Notifies a separation between different portions of a message	Can be used where there is no clear distinction between different parts of the message
BREAK BREAK	Indicates the separation between messages to different aircraft	
CANCEL	Annul the previously transmitted clearance	

Word/Phrase	Meaning	Notes
CHECK	Examine a system or procedure	No response is normally expected to this instruction
CLEARED	Authorised to proceed under the conditions specified	
CONFIRM	I request verification of a clearance, instruction, action or information	
CORRECT	True or accurate	
DISREGARD	Ignore	
MAINTAIN	Continue in accordance with the conditions specified	Can also be used in the literal sense – eg "*Maintain VFR*"
NEGATIVE	No, or Permission is not granted, or That is not correct, or Not capable	
OUT	This exchange of transmissions is ended and I **do not** expect a response	Rarely used in normal communications
OVER	My transmissions is over and I **do** expect a response	Rarely used in normal communications
READ BACK	Repeat all, or a specified part, of this message exactly as received	
RECLEARED	A change has been made to your last clearance, this new clearance supersedes your previous clearance or part of it	
REPORT	Pass me the following information	
REQUEST	I would like to know, or I want to obtain	
ROGER	I have received all of your last transmission	This only means the message has been received, it does not mean the message will be acted upon and must not be used in place of Affirm or Negative.
STANDBY	Wait and I will call you	No response is expected and no form of clearance or permission is granted (or denied) by this phrase
UNABLE	I cannot comply with your request, instruction or clearance	When this word is used, a reason should normally be given
WILCO	Understood, will comply	Abbreviated from "**Will Co**mply", should not be used where a 'read back' is required (as described shortly).

These standard words and phrases are used in radio communications together with normal 'plain language' to construct messages and to understand instructions and information given. In all of the following examples of radio communications, letters and numbers are used in place of the full phonetic word or pronunciation, and the reader should assume the normal phonetic words and pronunciations apply.

 *"G-ED, backtrack **approved**"*

('Backtrack' means to taxi along the runway in the opposite direction to the take-off/landing direction)

 *"D-PL continue straight ahead **break break** Global 374 cleared to pushback"*

 *"F-MB **check** gear down and locked"*

 *"Mega 693 runway 09 **cleared** for take-off"*

 *"Cessna KN **check** altimeter setting and **confirm** level 70"*

 *"G-BO **disregard** last message, **break, maintain** heading 090"*

 *"M-DU **read back** clearance"*

 *"I-JK cross runway 17 **report** vacated"*

 *"FT **request** number of persons on board"*

 *"Station calling Southend Approach, **standby**"*

Figure 3.5a
Definitions of Clearance, Instruction and Information.

 *"Avon 92 **unable** to approve requested runway due landing traffic"*

Message Element	Pilot action	Detail
Clearance	Requires strict compliance	Clearances are usually transmitted by Air Traffic Control only. They need to be read-back and are to be strictly complied with.
Instruction	To be followed and carried out where safe and practically possible to do so	Instructions, in most cases, should be read back and are to be complied with where it is safe and practical to do so.
Information	Items of benefit for the pilot in the interests of safety	Information is provided to assist the safe conduct of the flight and should not be read back.

This is a good place to emphasise that if the pilot is in any way uncertain or confused about the meaning of a radio message, it is essential to raise that concern and not allow ambiguity or confusion to exist. This principle can be summed-up in the time-honoured aviation maxim:

If in doubt, shout

What follows are extended examples of the use of standard phraseology covering different phases of a VFR flight and incorporating different circumstances. There are also longer 'transcripts' of sample radio communications in the appendices to this publication.

Departure: The format of the initial call from an aircraft wanting to depart the airfield will vary with circumstances. The simplest way to make an initial call on a radio frequency is to use the call sign of the aeronautical station being called, then the aircraft's full call sign:

 "Perth Tower, EI-OOR"

In reply, the aeronautical station can give its own call sign and acknowledge the calling aircraft as an invitation to establish two-way communication:

 "EI-OOR, Perth Tower"

In circumstances where the pilot is certain that its transmission will be received (for example, if you are parked next to the tower!), the pilot may make an initial call including a message, for example a request for information:

 "Perth Tower, EI-OOR, request airfield information"

 "EI-OOR, Perth Tower, QNH is 998 hectopascals, runway in use is 03, surface wind 050 7"

"QNH 998 hectopascals, runway 03, EI-OOR"

The exact format of an initial call from an aircraft to an aeronautical station is often a source of confusion and considerable debate amongst pilots. As is often the case, it is best to keep things simple and when constructing an initial call there are really just three important pieces of information to communicate:

Who you are;

Where you are;

What you want.

Here is an example of an aircraft making an initial call at the beginning of a flight, remembering that in the initial call the full call sign of both the aircraft and the aeronautical station should be used:

"Calais Tower,

[Who] *F-HLRA, DA-42,*

[Where] *on the main apron,*

[What] *request taxi for VFR flight to Rouen"*

You can expect that in this instance, the station being called will respond with information and – because this is the call sign for an Air Traffic Control (ATC) service – some form of clearance or instruction. What follows is a full sequence of calls for an aircraft departing from Calais.

 "Calais Tower, F-HLRA, DA-42, on the main apron, ready to taxi for VFR flight to Rouen"

"F-HLRA, Calais Tower, QNH 1003, runway 24 left, taxi to holding point C"

"QNH 1003, runway 24L, taxi to holding point C, F-HLRA"

"F-HLRA, holding point C. Ready for departure, request backtrack"

"F-RA, Runway 24 left, cleared to enter, backtrack and line-up"

"Cleared to enter and backtrack Runway 24 left, F-RA"

"Ready for departure, F-RA"

"F-RA, Runway 24 left cleared for take-off"

Note: The words "*take-off*" are first used only when an aircraft is cleared for take-off by ATC. At all other times the word "*departure*" is used. Thus, the words "*take-off*" are first used by Air Traffic Control, and then acknowledged by the aircraft.

When departing an airfield with Air Traffic Control, the aircraft will usually be given some form of departure routing to be followed. If the departure airfield is inside controlled airspace, a VFR departure clearance is likely to include a specific point at which to leave controlled airspace and some form of level instruction or restriction. In accordance with the read-back rules, such a departure clearance must be read-back in full. ATC will use the aircraft's full call sign when issuing a departure clearance. Because a departure clearance is NOT a clearance to take-off, ATC may emphasise the point:

"G-PA ready for departure"

"G-LTPA, hold position. After departure climb straight ahead to altitude 2500ft, QNH 1025, then turn left to leave the zone at Anytown, maintain VFR"

"Holding. After departure climb straight ahead to altitude 2500ft, QNH 1025, then turn left to leave the zone at Anytown, maintain VFR. G-LTPA"

Figure C3.6

A runway extended centreline – an extension of the runway centreline beyond the runway itself.

If ATC give a departure clearance to depart 'straight ahead' after take-off, this means that the aircraft should track the runway extended centre-line after take-off, until the specified point/level.

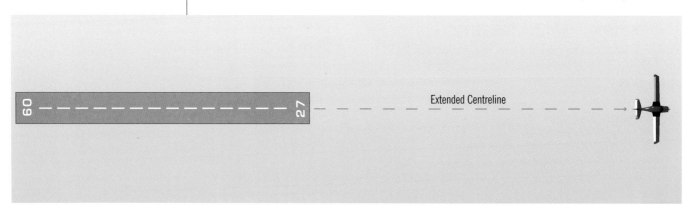

Extended Centreline

At times, ATC may require an aircraft to line-up on the runway and hold position awaiting clearance to take-off. In this situation, ATC may use the instruction 'wait' to emphasise that the aircraft has not been cleared to take-off:

 *"D-NV, Runway 03, line-up and **wait**"*

 *"Line-up and **wait** Runway 03, D-NV"*

Conversely, to maintain separation between aircraft ATC may sometimes need an aircraft to take-off straight away. This is one reason why a pilot should never report 'ready for departure' until both the aircraft and the pilot are actually ready to take-off. To emphasise that take-off needs to start without delay, ATC will use the word 'immediate':

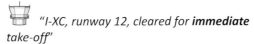 *"I-XC, runway 12, cleared for **immediate** take-off"*

 *"Runway 12, cleared for **immediate** take-off, I-XC"*

If an aircraft is at a runway holding point when the pilot accepts an 'immediate take-off' clearance, the aircraft is expected to taxi onto the runway and take-off without stopping. If the aircraft is already lined-up on the runway, once an 'immediate' clearance has been accepted, it is expected to take-off straight-away. Of course, a pilot always has the option to refuse such a clearance, and ATC may emphasis this by confirming an alternative option:

 *"Eagle 17, runway 23, take-off immediately or hold short of runway"*

 "Holding, Eagle 17"

To expedite traffic flow, ATC may also issue a '**conditional clearance**' so that, for example, a clearance to enter a runway is conditional on another aircraft landing first. Conditional clearances are only issued when the aircraft or vehicles involved are visible at all times to both the controller and the pilot. Further, the aircraft or vehicle which is the subject of the condition must be the first one that will pass the aircraft being offered the clearance. A conditional clearance must be given in a specific order and specific format, that order and format is:

- The call sign
- The condition
- The clearance
- A brief reiteration of the condition

It is essential that the pilot fully understands the condition and, for example, is absolutely certain of the identification of the aircraft or vehicle that is the subject of the condition. As always, the pilot should not hesitate to request clarification of any information, clearance or instruction if he or she has any uncertainty. Here is an example of a conditional clearance:

 *"Piper MA, behind the landing A320, line-up runway 15, behind"*

 "Behind the landing A320, line-up runway 15, behind, Piper MA"

There is also standard phraseology which applies to **helicopters** specifically, where the term 'taxi' is replaced with 'air-taxi'. For example:

 *"G-RT, **air-taxi** to flying club apron via taxiway B"*

 *"**Air-taxi** to flying club via taxiway B, G-RT"*

Climb and descent clearances: Once an aircraft is airborne, it may continue to receive ATC instructions and clearances (especially if it is inside controlled airspace), for example to change level:

 *"D-NY, **climb** to altitude 4500 feet"*

*"**Climb** to altitude 4500 feet, D-NY"*

'Climb' means to climb to and maintain the cleared level (descend means to descend to and maintain the cleared level). Normally, an aircraft is expected to begin the climb or descent as soon as the clearance has been acknowledged. If the aircraft can carry-out the climb or descent at its own convenience, ATC may use the phrase 'when ready', for example:

*"F-ZE, **when ready**, climb to altitude 3000 feet"*

ATC may also qualify a climb (or descent) clearance with an additional requirement, for example:

"F-ZE, climb to altitude 7500 feet, report passing 5000 feet"

"F-ZE, descend to altitude 2500 feet, expedite descent until passing 3500 feet"

En-route: During the 'en-route' phase of the flight, a VFR flight may operate in different classes of airspace and receive different levels of service from different Air Traffic Service Units (ATSU). It is worth re-iterating that the suffix of the ATSU's call sign will indicated what sort of service it is providing. As a general rule, clearances and instructions in the en-route phase of a VFR flight can only be issued by Air Traffic Control units, which are indicated by call signs such as 'Tower', 'Approach', 'Zone', 'Control'.

An ATSU with the call sign 'information' is providing a Flight Information Service as previously described, and is generally only able to issue information (and maybe advice).

An ATSU with the call sign 'Radio' can offer neither an ATC nor information service.

As a default, within European airspace an aircraft receiving either an Air Traffic Control or Flight Information Service is also receiving an **alerting service**. An alerting service is a service provided to notify the appropriate organisations if an aircraft is in need of search and rescue aid, and assist such organisations as required. In other words, if you suffer some sort of emergency whilst using an ATC or Flight Information Service, or go missing (for example, if you stop responding to radio calls) the ATC or FIS unit will take responsibility for alerting the appropriate agencies to locate and if necessary rescue the aircraft occupants.

If an aircraft remains on the same frequency for a long period of time without making any transmissions, the ATSU may become concerned that contact has been lost. Therefore an aircraft is required to make radio contact with the ATSU between 20 to 40 minutes after the last transmission. One option is to transmit the aircraft's call sign and the words *"operations normal"*. This is particularly important if the aircraft is operating over particularly remote or inhospitable terrain.

Occasionally, an ATSU may make a general broadcast to all aircraft on frequency, using the words *"all stations"*. No reply is expected to an 'all stations' transmission.

Arrival: On arrival at the destination, it will be necessary to obtain information about the aerodrome and conditions, to obtain information on any other traffic around the aerodrome, to integrate into any established traffic pattern and position to land. At some airfields, there may be automated broadcasts of airfield information (these are described more fully later in this publication). Where this facility does not exist, the airfield ATSU should pass the essential information to the arriving flight, including:

- Any specific joining or routing instructions
- The runway in use
- The surface wind
- The pressure setting (QNH and/or QFE)
- Details of any traffic

The following example assumes that the aircraft is already on the airfield's frequency (for example, it is returning from a local flight):

"Fairfield Tower, G-HF overhead Springfield altitude 2000 feet for landing"

"G-HF, roger. Join downwind left-hand for runway 12, surface wind 130 degrees 10 knots, QNH 1008, no reported traffic"

"Join downwind left-hand for runway 12, QNH 1008, roger, G-HF"

Methods for **joining the visual circuit** (or visual pattern) at an airfield vary between different states and there is no single internationally accepted protocol, other than the overriding procedure that an arriving aircraft is required to conform to any established pattern being used by other traffic at the airfield – unless ATC authorise a different routing.

The Visual Circuit: The visual circuit around the landing runway in use most often consists of a rectangle, with left-hand turns as standard and the following key points:

Figure C3.7
The visual circuit, in this case right-hand.

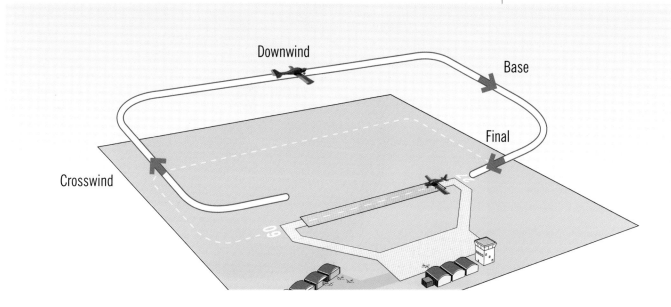

Where a circuit is right-hand, or the circuit direction is variable, the direction will always be specified by the ATSU.

The circuit is also sometimes referred to as the 'pattern'. At some airfields (in particular military airfields), the visual circuit may be flown as a 'racetrack' pattern, turning continuously from climb-out to downwind, then making a single turn from the end of downwind onto final approach.

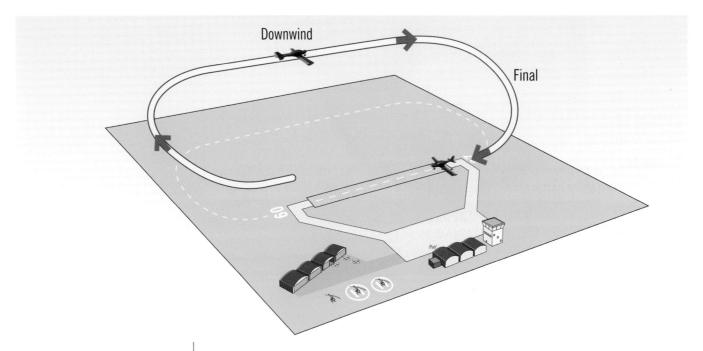

Figure C3.8
An alternative visual circuit, flown as a 'racetrack' shape and often used at military airfields.

The term "*final*" applies to a **final approach** lined up to the landing runway and within four miles of the runway. If an aircraft turns onto final approach at more than 4nm from the runway, or passes 8 miles to the landing runway on a straight-in approach, that part of the approach is referred to as "*long final*". If an aircraft makes a 'long final' report, a further 'final' report is required when the aircraft is at 4 miles from the runway.

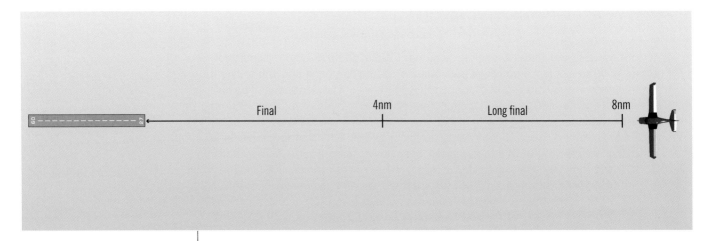

Figure C3.9
An aircraft lined up with the runway to land can report "*Final*" at up to four nautical miles from the runway, or "*Long Final*" if between 4 and 8 nautical miles from the runway.

The visual circuit itself is a place where aircraft tend to congregate and so both the pilots of those aircraft and the ATSU will be seeking an orderly flow of traffic and no conflicts between aircraft. To maintain traffic flow and separation, ATC may specify an order for landing, and all aircraft are required to maintain that order, for example:

 "F-KU downwind"

 *"F-KU, **number two**, follow the Cessna 172 on base leg"*

 *"**Number two**, Cessna in sight, F-KU"*

The two standard locations in the visual circuit for making a position report are downwind (or late downwind) and final, however the ATSU may require an additional or non-standard position report:

 "G-EW downwind"

 "G-EW, roger, report on base"

 "Wilco, G-EW"

 "D-JV downwind"

 "D-JV, number two, extend downwind and report before turning base, number one on four mile final"

 "Number two, wilco, D-JV"

Landing: When an aircraft reports 'final', an ATC unit will give the pilot some form of clearance. A clearance to land will include the runway designation and the surface wind:

 "I-VL final"

 *"I-VL, surface wind 200 degrees, 10 knots, **runway 21 cleared to land**"*

 *"**Runway 21 cleared to land**, I-VL"*

If some factor means that a landing clearance cannot be given straight away, the aircraft may be cleared to continue the approach, pending a further clearance. If an ATC unit does this, a reason will usually be given:

 "G-PT final"

 *"G-PT, **continue approach**, vehicle crossing runway"*

 *"**Continue approach**, G-PT"*

A further clearance is to be expected either for the aircraft to land, or to 'go around'.

A visual **go around** – sometimes known as a 'missed approach' – is a manoeuvre where an aircraft on final approach (or in the landing manoeuvre itself) breaks off the approach or landing and climbs back to the circuit height, usually while positioning to the 'deadside' of the runway – that is, the side opposite to the established circuit pattern.

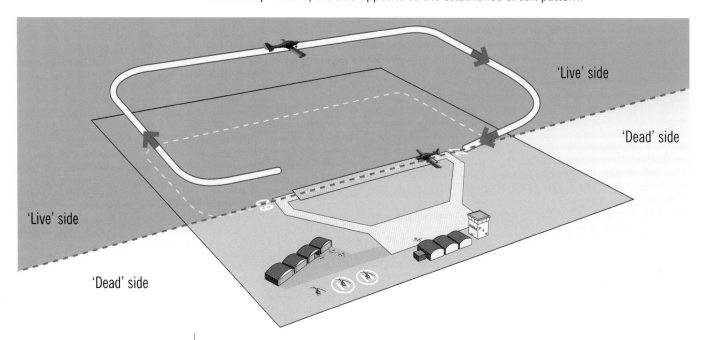

Figure C3.10
The 'Live Side' of the circuit is that side of the runway in use where the circuit pattern is active. The opposite side of the runway is the 'Dead Side'. In this case (a right-hand circuit), the airspace to the right of the runway – as viewed in direction of take-off and landing – is 'live side'. The airspace to the left is 'dead side'.

If the pilot knows that an approach is planned to finish with a go-around, this should be reported in good time to allow other pilots and the ATSU to plan accordingly:

 "M-BU final, go around"

 "M-BU, Runway 27 cleared low approach go around on deadside"

 "Runway 27 cleared low approach, wilco M-BU"

ATC may also initiate a go around:

 *"City475, **go around**, climb straight ahead"*

 *"**Going around**, wilco, City475"*

Another common training manoeuvre is the **touch and go**, in which an aircraft lands, continues rolling along the runway, and makes another take-off without stopping. Again, the ATSU and other pilots need to know if this is the intention:

 *"G-QV final, **touch and go**"*

 *"G-QV, runway 07 cleared **touch and go**, surface wind calm"*

 *"Runway 07 cleared **touch and go**, G-QV"*

If an aircraft has been making a series of touch and goes, it is helpful to let the ATSU and other pilots know when planning a 'full stop' landing:

 "D-YT downwind, to land"

 "D-YT roger, report final"

Vacating the runway: An ATSU will generally avoid transmitting to an aircraft during periods such as take-off and landing. Nevertheless, it may be necessary to pass instructions to an aircraft that has just landed in relation to where to leave – **vacate** – the runway. For example:

 "Diamond VN take the next left"

Or

 "Diamond VN take the next convenient right"

If the ATSU wants the aircraft to move off the runway as quickly as possible, it may instruct the aircraft to 'expedite', for example:

 *"Diamond VN **expedite** vacating"*

In any of the above instances, the pilot should remember the overriding order of priorities:

Aviate : Navigate : Communicate

If what ATC are asking you to do is not possible (maybe you are going too fast to make the next exit), or trying to comply with the clearance would involve unacceptable risk (for example heavy braking on a slippery runway), the pilot must make the safety of their aircraft the number one priority, and in due course inform ATC that they cannot comply with the clearance, for example:

 "Diamond VN unable to vacate next left due runway state"

Wake Turbulence: When operating around larger aircraft the avoidance of **wake turbulence** becomes an important consideration. On departure, ATC will not normally issue a take-off clearance until the appropriate wake turbulence separation has been achieved, for example:

 "D-CO ready for departure"

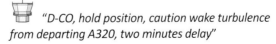 *"D-CO, hold position, caution wake turbulence from departing A320, two minutes delay"*

 "Holding D-CO"

If a light aircraft is making a visual approach behind a larger aircraft, ATC may again warn of the danger of wake turbulence:

"F-SH, runway 24 cleared visual approach, maintain own separation from preceding Boeing 757, caution wake turbulence"

Aerodrome Flight Information Service (AFIS): So far the examples of standard phraseology have focussed on terms which may be used by an ATC unit. At an **AFIS unit**, some phraseology will be different as the unit is only offering advice and information – not clearances or instructions. In principle the AFIS unit will provide information about the airfield (pressure settings, runway in use etc) and details of any known traffic, but it is the pilot's responsibility to decide how to proceed.

 "Marton Information, Wearside 17 request departure information"

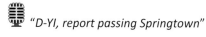 *"Wearside 17 Runway 24, wind 220 5 knots, QNH 1011"*

 "Runway 24, QNH 1011 Wearside 17"

 "Wearside 17, ready for departure"

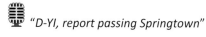 *"Wearside 17, wind 210 7 knots, runway 24 is free"*

 "Will take-off runway 24, Wearside 17"

Alternatively, an AFIS may use a slightly different phraseology:

 "Wearside 17, ready for departure"

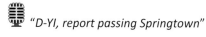 *"Wearside 17, no reported traffic runway 24, wind 210 7 knots"*

 "Will line-up runway 24, Wearside 17"

If there is traffic, the AFIS will advise but will not issue instructions to the pilot:

 "Wearside 17, ready for departure"

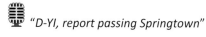 *"Wearside 17, runway occupied and landing traffic one mile final"*

 "Holding, Wearside 17"

When communicating with airborne traffic, the AFIS can once again provide information, and make a request of the pilot, but not issue clearances or instructions:

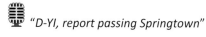 *"D-YI, report passing Springtown"*

 "Wilco D-YI"

 "D-YI passing Springtown and changing to Rhineback approach"

When an aircraft is arriving at an airfield with AFIS, the same principles apply:

 "Retley Information, F-HJKL"

 "F-HJKL, Retley Information"

 "F-HJKL overhead Banksly, 1800 feet, for landing"

 "F-KL, runway 33 left-hand circuit, wind 300 10 knots, QNH 1017, one aircraft in the circuit, report downwind"

 "Runway 33, QNH 1017, wilco F-KL"

 "F-KL, Downwind"

 "F-KL, roger, traffic is a Cessna 152 on base, report on base"

 "F-KL, traffic in sight, wilco"

 "F-KL, base"

 "F-KL, roger, report final"

 "F-KL, wilco"

 "F-KL, final"

 "F-KL, roger, no reported traffic runway 33"

 "F-KL, will land runway 33"

"F-KL, runway vacated"

 "F-KL, taxiway A available to flying school"

"Will taxi to the flying school via taxiway A, F-KL"

C33

Items requiring read back

You may have noticed in the preceding examples of radio messages that some items from ATSU messages are repeated back by the pilot – this is called a **read back**. In a message from an ATSU to an aircraft, there are certain specified items of information, clearances or instructions that are so important that they need to be 'read-back' by the pilot to ensure that they have been correctly received. The ATSU will not prompt the pilot to do this, unless the pilot fails to do so in which case he or she can expect a reminder. Of course, reading-back information or clearances is a lot easier if you've had the foresight to write them down in the first place and those operating an Air Traffic Service Unit (ATSU) are generally good at not passing detailed clearances and instructions during critical phases of flight or when the pilot is likely to be concentrating on a complex taxiing route, for example. If an ATSU does want to pass on some detailed but non-urgent information at an inconvenient moment, there is nothing wrong with the pilot telling them to 'Standby' until ready to take the message.

These are the items of information, instructions or clearances that are to be read-back in full:

Information, instructions or clearances that require a read-back
• Altimeter Settings (including units when value is below 1000 hectopascals)
• Runway **in Use**
• Airways or Route Clearances
• SSR (transponder) Instructions
• Taxi/Towing Instructions
• Clearance to Enter, Land On, Take-Off On, Backtrack, Cross, or Hold Short of any active runway
• Level Instructions
• Heading Instructions
• Speed Instructions
• Frequency Changes
• Type of Air Traffic Service
• **Transition Levels**
• **Approach Clearances**
• VDF Information

Figure C3.11
Information, instructions and clearances which must be read-back.

This is a good place to re-emphasise that if you are not sure that you have heard or understood an item of information, a clearance or an instruction properly, remember the basic principle of aviation communications:

If in doubt, shout

Here are some examples of 'read-back' in action, the items requiring read-back are in bold:

 "Scatsta Tower, F-HLRA, DA-42, on the North apron, request taxi for VFR flight to Lerwick"

 *"F-HLRA, Scatsta Tower. **Runway 24, QNH 1024** surface wind 300 degrees 12 knots. **Taxi holding point A**"*

 *"F-HLRA, **Runway 24, QNH 1024. Taxi holding point A**"*

---

 *"Sparrow 9. After departure your clearance is to **leave the zone via Hethel, VFR, not above 2,500ft QNH 998 hectopascals**"*

 *"After departure **cleared to leave the zone via Hethel, VFR, not above 2,500ft QNH 998 hectopascals,** Sparrow 9"*

Note: a departure clearance, as shown above, is NOT a clearance to take-off, that clearance will be given separately.

 *"Mainair 761, **squawk 5432**"*

 *"**Squawk 5432,** Mainair 761"*

Note: more details on Secondary Surveillance Radar (SSR) – transponder – operation are given in the following chapter.

---

 *"Piper JT, surface wind 220 14, **Runway 24 cleared for take-off**"*

 *"**Runway 24 cleared for take-off**, Piper JT"*

---

 *"G-HV **cross Runway 31**, report vacated"*

 *"**Cross Runway 31**, wilco, G-HV"*

---

 *"Spanhoe 17, surface wind 090, **Runway 11, cleared to land**"*

 *"**Runway 11, cleared to land**, Spanhoe 17"*

---

 *"G-AZ **maintain Flight Level 60, turn left heading 130**"*

 *"**Maintain Flight Level 60, turn left heading 130** G-AZ*

"M-RI call **Stansted Approach 120.625**"

 "**Stansted Approach 120.625**, M-RI"

 "Alpha 1 identified, **radar control service**"

 "**Radar control service**, Alpha 1"

 "N71B **climb flight level 100, transition altitude 6000**"

 "**Climb flight level 100, transition altitude 6000**, N71B"

 "D-MA, **cleared final number one**"

"**Cleared final number one**, D-MA"

"G-KX, request QDM, G-KX"

 "G-KX, **QDM 170 degrees, class 2**"

 "**QDM 170 degrees, class 2**, G-KX"

Note: The use of VHF Direction Finding (VDF) is described in the 'National Procedures' section.

Transfer of communications

Once a pilot has established communications with an ATSU on a particular frequency, it is wrong to leave that frequency without notifying the ATSU, so there is no doubt as to whether the aircraft is still in two-way communication with that ATSU. As a general rule **transfer of communications** is initiated by the ATSU if the aircraft is receiving an Air Traffic Control (ATC) service, but can be suggested by the ATSU or initiated by the pilot when the aircraft is receiving an information or radio service.

There are two key instructions used by ATC when instructing a pilot to change frequency:

Word	Meaning
CONTACT	Establish communications with [call sign] [frequency]....
MONITOR	Listen out on [call sign] [frequency]....

Figure C3.12

Standard phraseology used when transferring communications between ATSUs.

In accordance with the 'read back' protocols, a change of frequency is one of those items which has to be read back by the pilot. In addition, it is sensible to write-down the new frequency in order to be absolutely sure you have noted it correctly.

 *"F-VT, **contact Lille Approach 126.475**"*

 *"**Contact Lille Approach 126.475**, F-VT"*

As a reminder, the 'default' protocol with radio frequencies is that all digits of the frequency are transmitted, except if the fifth and sixth digits are both zero, in which case they can be omitted. The decimal place is transmitted as 'decimal' (pronounced as *"Day See Mal"*).

Aircraft flying in controlled airspace (and so, by definition, receiving some form of ATC service) must not change frequency without permission from ATC.

When a frequency change is instructed by ATC, it is normally expected that the pilot will make contact on the new frequency straight away. Occasionally, ATC may leave the timing of the frequency change to the discretion of the pilot:

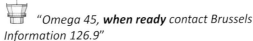 *"Omega 45, **when ready** contact Brussels Information 126.9"*

 *"**When ready** Brussels Information 126.9, Omega 45"*

A frequency change may be initiated by the pilot, for example, when the flight is receiving an Information or radio service.

 "London Information, D-PI, changing to Jersey Control 125.2"

Once the pilot has set the new frequency on the radio, the first task is – do nothing. Whenever changing onto a new frequency, the pilot should listen out for at least a few seconds to reduce the risk of interrupting an on-going conversation or transmitting 'over the top' of another transmission. Few things are more frustrating to controllers and pilots alike than a pilot suddenly appearing on frequency, broadcasting their life history unannounced and so interrupting an important radio exchange.

Once satisfied that a transmission will not interrupt an on-going conversation, the pilot should start with a simple opening transmission. Often all that is required is the name of the station being addressed and the aircraft's call sign.

 "Lille Information, G-VPSJ"

It may the case that the ATSU already has details of your flight (maybe passed on by the previous ATSU) and so there is no need to give all your information

 *"G-SJ, Lille Information, **I have your details**, report passing Cap Gris-Nez"*

"Wilco G-SJ"

Alternatively the ATSU may invite the pilot to pass the flight details, either by simply giving its call sign, or optionally by using the phrase 'pass your message'.

 "G-SJ, Lille Information"

 *"G-SJ, Lille Information, **pass your message**"*

The exact format of a message passing the aircraft's flight details to a new ATSU will depend upon the circumstances at the time. An aircraft returning to its base airfield after a local sortie may only need to give basic details of the pilot's intentions or a request for information.

 "Strubby Radio, G-WARB"

 "G-RB, Strubby Radio"

 "G-RB, inbound for landing, 5 miles south of the airfield at 1500 feet, request airfield information"

If the aircraft is in the 'en-route' phase of a VFR flight, and the unit contacted does not have the aircraft's flight details, the basic items of information the ATSU will want to know are:

- **Who** you are
- **Where** you are
- **What** you want

A good format for passing en-route VFR flight details, in common usage, is:

T – aircraft callsign and **T**ype

P – **P**oint of departure and destination, present **P**osition

A – **A**ltitude/height/flight level, with altimeter setting if appropriate

I – **I**ntentions/**I**nformation eg flight profile, estimate for next turning point etc.

R – flight **R**ules, **R**equest, **R**outing, further information etc.

For those who like mnemonics, this format can be remembered as 'TP AIR'. For example:

 "Halfpenny Green Information, G-BGLH"

 "G-LH, Halfpenny Green Information, pass your message"

"G–LH,

[Type]...*Cessna 152*

[Point of departure/destination, position]...*from Hawarden to Shoreham, overhead Telford...*

[Altitude]...*2800 feet, QNH 1032...*

[Intentions/information]...*ETA overhead Halfpenny Green 25...*

[Rules, Request]...*VFR, request Halfpenny Green QNH"*

If the ATSU cannot begin a conversation when the pilot first calls, the pilot may be requested to 'standby'.

 "Lille Information, G-VPSJ"

 *" G-VPSJ, Lille Information, **standby**"*

As a recap, **standby** means 'Wait and I will call you', a response is not expected and no permission or clearance is granted by the phrase (although 'Standby' is not a denial either). In particular, permission to enter controlled or regulated airspace requires a very specific clearance, the word 'standby' grants no such permission. The ATSU will call the pilot as soon as they are able to (they rarely forget).

Figure C3.13
A busy ATSU is likely to be undertaking a number of tasks at any one time, in addition to talking to pilots on the radio.

This is a good place to emphasise that an air traffic controller or other ATSU operator may well have other tasks on hand in addition to communicating on the frequency – for example liaising with other ATSUs, co-ordinating with other controllers at the unit or operational phone calls. In some cases, a controller may be operating two frequencies at the same time, so even if the radio frequency seems to be quiet, the controller or radio operator may be busy with other tasks.

If the pilot is unable to establish contact on a new frequency, the first step is to check that the correct frequency has been selected – which is one good reason for writing down frequency changes. If the pilot is still unable to establish contact, the usual protocol is to return to the previous frequency. If contact cannot be re-established on the previous frequency, an alternative frequency should be selected (which, thanks to good pre-flight planning, you should have to hand of course).

Transponder operating procedures

A transponder is a piece of aircraft equipment which allows the aircraft to be 'seen' by ATC **Secondary Surveillance Radar** (SSR). In essence, a signal (interrogation) is broadcast from the ground and the aircraft's transponder replies with specified information. This information is displayed to the Air Traffic Controller on a radar screen at the aircraft's position. Because SSR operates on common frequencies, the aircraft's transponder 'return' can be viewed by any suitably equipped ATC unit within range – it is not necessary for the aircraft to be in voice communication with an ATC unit for that unit to be able to see the aircraft's transponder information. Out-of-interest, some of this information can also be viewed via publically-accessible websites and apps.

Figure C3.14

A typical transponder for General Aviation aircraft. All modern transponders have the 'ALT' altitude reporting feature, sometimes known as 'Mode C'.

The Standardised Rules of the Air (SERA) require that if an aircraft has a serviceable transponder, it should be operated at all times during a flight – regardless of whether the aircraft is in airspace where the carriage of transponders is mandatory.

At its most basic usage, the ATC units will see the four-digit code selected by the pilot on the transponder. Virtually all transponders also have a feature usually marked on the transponder as 'ALT' – when this is selected the aircraft's level will also be broadcast. Under SERA, anytime the transponder is in use, the ALT feature must also be selected if it is available. The ALT feature is sometimes also known by its original name of 'Mode C'.

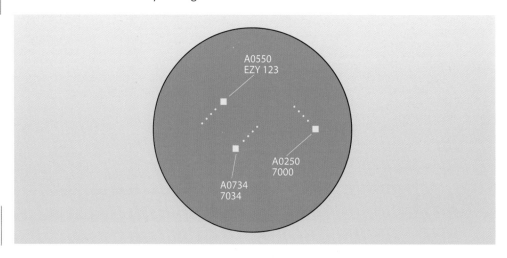

Figure C3.15

A typical ATC radar display showing transponder information from aircraft.

The current generation of transponders ('Mode S') can also broadcast additional information, for example the aircraft's registration.

An ATC unit which has SSR capability will be allocated a range of transponder codes and in normal VFR flight, it will often be necessary to change transponder codes when transferring between different ATC units. Instructions in relation to transponder codes use the term **squawk**. For example *"Squawk 4756"* means to select the code 4756 on the aircraft's transponder, and ensure that the correct mode is selected.

Normally, each digit of the transponder code is transmitted individually, although the word 'thousand' may be used if the number is a round thousand, for example:

Transponder Code	Transmitted as
4756	*"Squawk four seven five six"*
7000	*"Squawk seven thousand"*

Figure C3.16

The transmission of a transponder code ('squawk').

Figure C3.17

Standard phraseology for the operation of the transponder.

Here is the standard SSR/Transponder phraseology:

Phrase	Meaning	Notes
Squawk [code] [mode]	Set the specified transponder code as instructed.	Unless instructed otherwise, pilots should always select 'Altitude' mode (ALT / Mode C) on, even if ATC do not specify the mode
Squawk Ident	Operate the 'Ident' function on the transponder	
Squawk Standby	Set the transponder to 'standby' mode	In this mode the transponder does not transmit
Squawk Charlie	Select the 'Altitude /Mode C' function on the transponder	
Squawk Altitude	Select the 'Altitude /Mode C' function on the transponder	
Squawk Mayday	Select the Emergency transponder code	This code is 7700
Confirm squawk	Confirm the code / mode selected on the transponder	The pilot is expected to: • Check the code setting on the transponder; • Reselect the code if necessary; and • Confirm to ATC the code and mode selected on the transponder
Reset Squawk[code]	Reselect the assigned transponder code	
Stop Squawk	Set the transponder to standby or off so that it is not transmitting	
Stop Squawk altitude	Deselect the altitude reporting function of the transponder	
Stop Squawk Charlie	Deselect the altitude reporting function of the transponder	
Stop Squawk altitude – wrong indication	Deselect the altitude reporting function of the transponder, the level readout is incorrect	
Stop Squawk Charlie – wrong indication	Deselect the altitude reporting function of the transponder, the level readout is incorrect	
Confirm [level]	Check and report your current level	
Check altimeter setting and confirm [level]	Check the selected pressure setting and confirm your current level	
Squawking [code] [mode]	My transponder is set to [code] [mode]	

All transponder operating instructions must be read-back by the pilot.

 *"Interair 56, **squawk 6432**"*

 *"**Squawk 6432**, Interair 56"*

 *"D-GA, **stop squawk altitude, wrong indication**"*

 *"**Stop squawk altitude**, D-GA"*

*"G-BV, **reset squawk 3470**"*

 *"**Resetting squawk 3470**, G-BV"*

When operating under an Air Traffic Control service, the transponder code to be used is that instructed by ATC. At other times, there are a small number of 'general' transponder codes which can be set without instruction from Air Traffic Control. These codes are sometimes known to the aviation authorities as **conspicuity** codes. 'Conspicuity' means clearly visible or attracting attention, although this word has yet to find its way into many non-aviation dictionaries.

Code	Meaning
7000	In most European airspace, 7000 is used as a non-specific 'conspicuity' code and should be selected whenever no other code has been specified by air traffic services. In many (but not all states), the '7000' code also indicates that the aircraft is operating under Visual Flight Rules (VFR). Is it not necessary to be in contact with an ATSU to squawk 7000
7004	Many European states specify this code to mean that an aircraft is performing aerobatic or air display manoeuvres

Figure C3.18
Standard transponder codes used in European airspace.

For exact transponder operating procedures in a state's airspace, the relevant Aeronautical Information Publication (AIP) should be consulted.

In addition to the 'conspicuity' codes, there are three internationally-recognised emergency transponder codes:

Code	Meaning	Notes
7700	Emergency	Generally only used if the aircraft is not already squawking a transponder code assigned by ATC
7600	Radio-communication failure	
7500	Unlawful interference with the planned operation of the flight	

Figure C3.19
The emergency transponder codes.

If an ATSU is providing some form of 'surveillance' service to a VFR flight – for example a Radar Control Service – it may issue information on other traffic to enable flight to maintain a safe separation. Before issuing such information, however, it will usually confirm that it has identified the aircraft:

"Tecnam AS, radar contact five miles north of Berwick"

"G-BV, identified 7 miles south of Compton"

When reporting traffic, an ATSU will usually use the 'clock code' to indicate the direction of other traffic in relation to the aircraft. The 'clock code' is based on the position of the hours on a watch face, 12 o'clock is straight ahead, 6 o'clock is directly behind; 3 o'clock is 90° to the right of straight ahead, 9 o'clock is 90° to the left of straight ahead.

Traffic may also be quantified in terms of 'high' or 'low' in relation to the aircraft, and in terms of direction of travel and distance. The following terms are used by ATC when reporting other traffic:

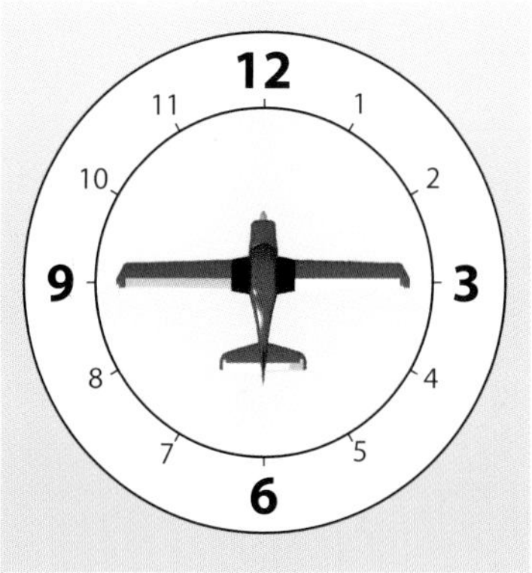

Traffic information terminology	Traffic information terminology
Unknown	Slow moving
Closing	Climbing
Opposite Direction	Descending
Same Direction	Aircraft type (if known)
Overtaking	Aircraft level (if known)
Crossing right to left	Clear of traffic
Crossing left to right	Resume own navigation
Fast moving	

Figure C3.20
The 'clock code' is used when reporting traffic, '12 o'clock' is straight ahead.

Figure C3.21
Standard phraseology used when reporting traffic.

The level of other traffic is generally only reported if the intentions of the traffic are known (for example, the other traffic is in contact with the same ATSU). If traffic information is based on observed information (for example, SSR altitude information), but its intentions are not known, level information may be reported as 'indicating', for example:

*"Princeair 17, traffic 11 o'clock, 1 mile, same direction, **indicating 600 feet above**"*

"D-XC, traffic two o'clock, 2 miles, opposite direction, 1000 feet below"

An ATSU may also report other traffic to an aircraft but advise *"Maintain own separation"*

An aircraft notified of other traffic can respond in a number of ways, depending on the circumstances:

 *"Looking out, G-AB"*

 "Traffic in sight, G-AB"

 "Negative contact [reasons], G-AB"

Once the other traffic is no longer potentially conflicting or relevant, the ATSU may report:

 "I-JK, clear of traffic, resume own navigation"

If an aeronautical station is not aware of any other traffic that will affect a flight, it may say so:

 "G-RU, no reported traffic"

Depending on the type of service being provided by the ATSU, it may give advice or instructions to avoid other traffic. A pilot can request avoiding action using the phrase 'Request vectors'

 "F-NR, request vectors"

 "F-NR, turn right heading 330 to avoid unknown traffic 11 o'clock two miles, closing, indicating same level"

If the ATSU uses the word 'immediately' when giving vectors or avoiding action, this implies a high level of urgency and the pilot should carry out the instruction immediately (if safe to do so), and only acknowledge once the action has been taken.

 *"Speedair 45, turn left **immediately** heading 330, traffic 1 o'clock, one mile, opposite direction, descending"*

The pilot must initiate the instruction first (if safe to do so) and only then acknowledge:

 "Left heading 330, Speedair 45"

Occasionally, after 'vectoring' a flight through a series of heading changes, the ATSU may then use the time-honoured phrase '**resume own navigation**' and maybe invite you to change frequency. If you are aware of your current location, and you are confident of the routing required to continue your flight as planned, this instruction is not a problem. However, if you have any doubt about your location, or the routing required to regain your original track or reach the next waypoint on your route, it is up to you to say so and request whatever navigation assistance you need. Make sure the ATSU provides the assistance you need until you are once again confident that you can proceed under your own VFR navigation – remember, they are there to help you! This is another example of the well-known proverb in relation to aviation communications:

If in doubt, shout

It is also worth knowing that even if a controller is providing vectors to an aircraft to avoid other traffic, the pilot of a VFR flight remains ultimately responsible for not colliding with other aircraft. Even when operating in class C and D controlled airspace, ATC clearances to a VFR flight do not imply any form of separation.

Not all urgent ATC instructions relate to aircraft in the air. In the following example, ATC need to cancel a take-off clearance that it has already given:

*"Diamond KL hold position, **cancel take-off** I say again **cancel take-off**, runway obstructed"*

"Holding, Diamond KL"

If an aircraft has commenced its take-off roll and for safety reasons its needs to abandon the take-off, ATC may issue an urgent instruction:

*"G-YT **stop immediately**, G-YT **stop immediately**"*

The pilot must initiate the instruction first (if safe to do so) and only then acknowledge:

"Stopping, G-YT"

Progress check

17. What is meant by 'readability 3'?
18. What category of radio message has priority over all others?
19. What is the correct meaning of the phrase 'Read back'?
20. What is the correct meaning of the phrase 'Roger'?
21. What is the correct meaning of the phrase 'Wilco'?
22. If you are positioned at the runway holding point, have completed all checks and are ready for take-off, what phrase should be used to communicate this situation to an ATSU?
23. What type of clearance is this: "*G-HU, behind the landing Cessna 172, line-up runway 23, behind*"?
24. What is the meaning of the ATC instruction 'descend'?
25. What is an aircraft's position if it reports 'long final?
26. What is an AFIS?
27. Name at least five items of information or instruction that are required to be 'read back' to the ATSU
28. What is the meaning of the phrase 'Contact'?
29. What is the meaning of the phrase 'standby' and what clearance can be granted with this phrase?
30. If an aircraft is fitted with a serviceable transponder, at what times during a flight should it be operated?
31. What is the meaning of the phrase 'Squawk ident'?
32. What is the meaning of the phrase 'Squawking'?
33. What information is transmitted by the transponder when Mode C/'ALT' is selected?
34. What is the standard European VFR 'conspicuity' code?
35. What is the transponder code which can be used to indicate that the aircraft has an emergency?
36. What 'clock code' might indicate that other traffic is slightly left of dead ahead of the aircraft?

These questions are intended to test knowledge and reinforce some of the key learning points from this section. In answering these questions, a 'pass rate' of about 80% should be the target.

Model answers are found at page C93

C4

Weather Information

ATIS and VOLMET broadcasts, Flight Information Service (FIS)

Progress check

7   **VOLMET Service**

Call Sign/ID	EM	Frequency MHz	Operating Hours	Stations	Contents	Remarks
				Table 3.5.7.1 — Meteorological Radio Broadcasts (VOLMET)		
1	2	3	4	5	6	7
London Volmet (Main)	A3E	135.375	H24 continuous	Amsterdam Brussels Dublin Glasgow London Gatwick London Heathrow London Stansted Manchester Paris/Charles de Gaulle	1. Half hourly reports (METAR) 2. The elements of each report broadcast in the following order: (a) Surface wind (b) Visibility (or CAVOK) (c) RVR if applicable (d) Weather (e) Cloud (or CAVOK)	The spoken word 'SNOCLO' will be added to the end of the aerodrome report when that aerodrome is unusable for take-offs and landings due to heavy snow on runways or runway snow clearance.
London Volmet (South)	A3E	128.600	H24 continuous	Birmingham Bournemouth Bristol Cardiff Jersey London Luton Norwich Southampton Southend Exeter	(f) Temperature (g) Dewpoint (h) QNH (i) Recent Weather if applicable (j) Windshear if applicable (k) TREND if applicable (l) Runway Contamination Warning if applicable	
London Volmet (North) **(Note 1)**	A3E	126.600	H24 continuous	Durham Tees Valley East Midlands Humberside Isle of Man Leeds Bradford Liverpool	3. Non-essential words such as 'surface wind', 'visibility' etc are not spoken. 4. Except for 'SNOCLO' (see Column 7), the Runway State Group is not broadcast.	

Weather Information

C4

ATIS and VOLMET broadcasts, Flight Information Service (FIS)

During almost any VFR flight, it is the weather that will be one of the most important variables which will determine the conduct and outcome of the flight. Any proficient pilot will check the forecast and actual weather as part of the flight planning process. Once the flight is underway, there are a number of ways of checking the weather and a sensible pilot will want to be aware of, and make use of, these cost-free resources.

Many larger airfields have a facility known as **Automatic Terminal Information Service – ATIS**. ATIS is an automated recorded broadcast of weather information for a specific airfield. An ATIS broadcast will include the current weather at the airfield, possibly together with other relevant information (runway in use, equipment unserviceability etc.). At a particularly busy airfield, there may be different ATIS broadcasts for departing and arriving aircraft. The ATIS is updated with each new weather report (usually every 30 minutes) and the broadcast will include the time of the weather observation and a code letter. A typical ATIS broadcast will sound like this:

> *"Dundee Information Echo, time 0720. Runway in use 27, surface wind 290 4knots. Visibility 10 kilometres or more, cloud few 1000 feet. Temperature +6, dewpoint +3, QNH 1019. Acknowledge receipt of information Echo and QNH 1019 on first contact with Dundee."*

When departing an airfield with an ATIS facility, the ATIS broadcast should be checked before first contact with the airfield ATSU. In that first contact, the pilot can confirm the receipt of the ATIS broadcast and the altimeter pressure setting, so that the ATSU does not have to repeat that information.

When arriving at an airfield, the ATIS broadcast is checked before making contact with the ATSU, once again this allows the pilot to plan ahead and avoids the ATSU having to repeatedly broadcast the airfield information to each arriving aircraft.

During the en-route phase of a flight an airfield's ATIS broadcast can also be useful to check that the weather is as expected, both at airfields along the route and at potential diversion airfields.

Figure C4.1

Details of ATIS broadcasts will be found in the Aeronautical Information Publication (AIP) and commercial flight guides.

EGJJ AD 2.18 AIR TRAFFIC SERVICES COMMUNICATION FACILITIES

Service Designation	Callsign	Channel(s)	Hours of Operation	Remarks
1	2	3	4	5
Air Traffic Control service	JERSEY CONTROL	125.200 MHz CTR and Airway Channel.	0545-2100 (0445-2030); and by arrangement.	DOC 4900N00100W - 4834N00205W - 4920N00400W - 5015N00400W - 5015N00145W - 4935N00100W / 25,000 ft.
	JERSEY CONTROL	120.450 MHz To be used in the event of failure of communications on 125.200 MHz.	0545-2100 (0445-2030); and by arrangement.	
APP	JERSEY APPROACH	120.300 MHz DOC 25 nm/10,000 ft.	0545-2100 (0445-2030); and by arrangement.	
	JERSEY APPROACH	118.550 MHz DOC 25 nm/10,000 ft.	0545-2100 (0445-2030); and by arrangement.	
	JERSEY APPROACH	121.500 MHz Emergency frequency.	0545-2100 (0445-2030); and by arrangement.	
TWR	JERSEY TOWER	119.450 MHz DOC 25 nm/4,000 ft.	0515-2100 (0415-2030); and by arrangement.	ATZ hours coincident with Approach hours.
	JERSEY GROUND	121.900 MHz DOC 2 nm/GND. GMC will be notified on ATIS.	As directed by ATC.	
ATIS	JERSEY INFORMATION	134.675 MHz DOC 60 nm/20,000 ft.	0545-2100 (0445-2030).	Tel: 01534-446301 for ATIS message.
Other	JERSEY FIRE	121.600 MHz Non-ATS frequency. DOC 2 nm/GND	Available when Fire vehicle attending aircraft on the ground in an emergency.	

ATIS frequencies are published in each countries Aeronautical Information Publication (AIP) as well as in commercial flight guides. As a general rule, ATIS is only updated during the published hours of operation of the airfield (or the hours specified in the AIP), so it pays to check the time of the ATIS broadcast carefully to make sure that it is not out-of-date.

Another aviation weather broadcast is **VOLMET** – a word apparently created by combining the French words for 'flight' (VOL) and for 'weather' (METeo). The word VOLMET is officially defined as meaning 'meteorological information for aircraft in flight'. In practice a VOLMET broadcast is an automated recorded broadcast of the weather reports (and sometimes weather forecasts) for a group of airfields located in broadly the same geographical area or Flight Information Region, for example:

London VOLMET (South)

Scottish VOLMET

Barcelona VOLMET

Stockholm VOLMET

Zurich VOLMET

Each VOLMET broadcast will transmit weather information for around 10 airfields, sometimes (but not always) in alphabetical order. As you might imagine, the entire broadcast is quite long and it is one of the unwritten laws of aviation that whenever you tune-in to a VOLMET broadcast, the airfield information you want has just been transmitted and you will have to wait for it to come around again. One of the advantages of VOLMET is that you may well be able to obtain an airfield's weather information while you are still well out-of-range of its ATIS broadcast. You may also be able to obtain weather information for en-route, destination and diversion airfields from a single broadcast, although you will still need to check an airfield's individual ATIS broadcast on arrival at that airfield.

Figure C4.2

Details of VOLMET broadcasts will be found in the appropriate Aeronautical Information Publication (AIP) and commercial flight guides.

VOLMET Service

Table 3.5.7.1 — Meteorological Radio Broadcasts (VOLMET)						
Call Sign/ID	EM	Frequency MHz	Operating Hours	Stations	Contents	Remarks
1	2	3	4	5	6	7
London Volmet (Main)	A3E	135.375	H24 continuous	Amsterdam Brussels Dublin Glasgow London Gatwick London Heathrow London Stansted Manchester Paris/Charles de Gaulle	1. Half hourly reports (METAR) 2. The elements of each report broadcast in the following order: (a) Surface wind (b) Visibility (or CAVOK) (c) RVR if applicable (d) Weather (e) Cloud (or CAVOK)	The spoken word 'SNOCLO' will be added to the end of the aerodrome report when that aerodrome is unusable for take-offs and landings due to heavy snow on runways or runway snow clearance.
London Volmet (South)	A3E	128.600	H24 continuous	Birmingham Bournemouth Bristol Cardiff Jersey London Luton Norwich Southampton Southend Exeter	(f) Temperature (g) Dewpoint (h) QNH (i) Recent Weather if applicable (j) Windshear if applicable (k) TREND if applicable (l) Runway Contamination Warning if applicable	
London Volmet (North) (Note 1)	A3E	126.600	H24 continuous	Durham Tees Valley East Midlands Humberside Isle of Man Leeds Bradford Liverpool London Gatwick Manchester Newcastle	3. Non-essential words such as 'surface wind', 'visibility' etc are not spoken. 4. Except for 'SNOCLO' (see Column 7), the Runway State Group is not broadcast. 5. All broadcasts are in English	

Details of VOLMET broadcasts, including hours of operation (usually 24 hours a day – H24), radio frequency, information broadcast and airfields covered (and in what order) can be found in the appropriate AIP as well as in commercial flight guides.

If you are unable to obtain an airfield's weather information from an ATIS or VOLMET broadcast, then in theory you can request an airfield's weather information from a Flight Information Service unit or other ATSU. In practice, the ability of an FIS unit or other ATSU to obtain weather information for a specific airfield is likely to be limited by factors such as controller workload. Controllers will always try to provide a service to pilots, but in some situations (such as a busy summer's weekend afternoon) the unit may simply not have the capacity to deal with non-urgent requests for weather information. That said, it is the job of ATSUs to provide information or assistance to pilots, so it is usually worth asking the question.

Progress check

37. What is an ATIS?
38. Where will the pilot find details of an ATIS broadcast?
39. What is the correct term for a recorded broadcast of weather reports for a group of airfields?

These questions are intended to test knowledge and reinforce some of the key learning points from this section. In answering these questions, a 'pass rate' of about 80% should be the target.

Model answers are found at page C94

Communications Failure

C5

Actions in the event of communication failure

Progress check

Light Signal	To an aircraft in flight
Steady green	Cleared to land
Steady red	Give way to other aircraft and continue circling
Series of green flashes	Return for landing (*)
Series of red flashes	Aerodrome unsafe, do not land
Series of white flashes	Land at this aerodrome and proceed to apron (*)
(*) Clearances to land and to taxi will be given in due course.v	

Communications Failure

Actions in the event of communication failure

Almost every modern aircraft, and for that matter the vast majority of vintage aircraft, carry some form of radio and make some form of voice communications during every flight. It can therefore be something of a shock if, for some reason, communications stop unexpectedly. Logically, the lack of voice communications does not alter the flying characteristics of any aircraft – it will perform just as it did before, the engine(s) will run just as well with or without radio, in Visual Meteorological Conditions (VMC) navigation should not be a major issue without voice communications.

What may change with a loss of voice communications is the choice of airfields and airspace that are available to the pilot, and extra considerations about integrating with existing traffic – especially if arriving 'non-radio' at an airfield that is not expecting your flight or where all other traffic is using radio.

However, before starting to consider **non-radio flight** in detail, the first actions in the event of an unexpected loss of voice communications should be some simple 'trouble-shooting' to see if communications can be restored. Most 'loss of communications' incidents involve some error or omission on the part of the pilot, which can usually be rectified by making some simple checks:

- Is the correct frequency selected? Were you previously communicating on this frequency or have you just changed to it? Are you sure the frequency is correct, are you within the normal hours of operation, should you be within range of the ground station? Can you hear any other transmissions on the frequency? Have you tried selecting an alternative frequency (for example the previous frequency)?

- Are the radio controls properly set-up? Is the volume set correctly? Is the frequency selected to 'active' (as opposed to 'standby')? Have you tried to establish communications on the second radio (if one is fitted)?

- If there is a separate 'audio controller', is this controller properly set so that your seat (left or right-hand) should be receiving and transmitting on the required frequency? Are the intercom controls properly set-up (including volume and any on/off selection)?

- Is the headset operating properly? Are any headset volume controls set correctly, is the headset fully plugged in (or has it been accidentally unplugged)? If the headset requires electrical power, has that run-out (for example, exhausted batteries)? If the headset is 'wireless' type, are all elements of the wireless system properly selected and working? Has the headset been checked in the sockets on the 'other side' of the cockpit, is there an alternative headset to check?

- If the aircraft has a separate 'Avionics Master Switch', has this been turned off accidentally?

- Is there a wider problem, such as an electrical failure?

While undertaking this troubleshooting, there must be an over-riding emphasis on maintaining the pilot's priorities:

Aviate : Navigate : Communicate

In other words the flying of the aeroplane, and knowing where you are and where you are going, must not be neglected whilst trying to sort out a potentially minor communications problem.

Even if you do decide that the aircraft's radio(s) has stopped working, there may still be other options for establishing contact with an ATSU. Many pilots carry hand-held radios (sometimes called portable transceivers) as a back-up for just such an eventuality – although obviously it is helpful if this is within reach of the pilot and not packed away in the baggage compartment, for example. It is worth remembering that a hand-held radio will almost certainly have less power (and so less range) than the radio fitted to the aircraft.

Additionally, virtually all pilots will have a mobile phone. Although in normal circumstances use of a mobile phone in the air is strongly discouraged, this is a situation where a mobile phone may prove useful in flight. Be aware, however, that the inside of the average light aircraft cockpit can be a very noisy place in flight, and conducting a mobile phone conversation in flight is likely to be challenging (although some headsets do have the facility to connect with mobile phones). The aircraft's altitude, and the terrain being overflown, will also have a bearing on the chances of establishing a mobile signal.

Once again, the tasks involved in trying to establish communications with a hand-held radio or mobile phone can distract the pilot from the primary task of flying the aeroplane, so it is important to reiterate the pilot's order of priorities:

Aviate : Navigate : Communicate

Having established that a communications failure has taken place, and having been unable to establish alternative voice communications, the pilot will need to make some decisions about how to continue the flight.

It may be the case that the planned flight only involves airspace and airfields where radio communication is not required, in which case the loss of communications may be nothing more than a minor inconvenience. Alternatively, a change of plan may be required. It is prudent to take a moment to 'take stock' of the situation, in particular:

- What is the fuel/range/endurance remaining?

- How much daylight remains?

- Are there any specific weather considerations?

- Is the radio failure part of a wider failure (or example, electrical system failure)?

It is not possible or sensible to give fixed advice which will fit every situation – a non-standard situation may require a flexible approach from the pilot, taking into account the circumstances prevailing. There are, however, a few procedural matters and guidelines to be considered for an aircraft which has suffered loss of communications:

- Remain in VMC if at all possible.

- Plan to land before sunset if at all possible.

- Use the 'radio failure' squawk (7600) if the transponder is operating.

- The aircraft must not enter controlled airspace without permission. Certain other airspace (for example Radio Mandatory Zones – RMZ) should also be avoided unless there is some overriding safety consideration.

- Where to land needs careful consideration. An airfield outside controlled airspace should be selected (if possible).

- The airfield (and traffic around it) may not be expecting your arrival – keep an especially good lookout and be prepared to 'give way' to other traffic that is unaware of your presence.

You may believe that your radio is transmitting but not receiving. In this case, you should make radio calls on the normal frequencies, stating your situation, position and intentions, and prefixing each radio call with the phrase, 'transmitting blind'. According to ICAO, a **Blind Transmission** is a transmission from one station to another station where two-way communication cannot be established but where it is believed that the station being called is able to receive the transmission. For example:

 "**Transmitting blind**, N34AM returning to the airfield for landing, 5 miles to the south, 2000ft QNH1016"

Alternatively, the radio may have failed so that it is receiving, but only 'carrier wave' (and not speech) is being transmitted. For this circumstance there is a 'Speechless Code', developed by the military but also understood at some civilian units. It involves pressing the 'Press To Talk' (PTT) button to make a short transmission. The Speechless Code is:

Number of short 'dashes'	Meaning
•	Yes
• •	No
• • •	Say Again
• • • •	Request Homing (eg a heading to fly to reach the airfield) or Request Assistance

Figure C5.1
The Speechless Code.

If you arrive at an airfield following a communications failure, the ATSU may (or may not) have the facility to make light signals. Be aware, however, that a report by accident investigators following a non-radio incident at a major airport concluded that light signals from the standard lamps that are (sometimes) found in an ATSU, may only be visible at up to about one nautical mile in good conditions – and probably less in conditions such as bright sunlight, or if filters are used, or if the light is shone through tinted windows in the control room. If you are arriving at an airfield where you expect to receive light signals from the tower, it may be sensible (other considerations permitting) to position on the 'dead side' of the circuit, close to the tower at circuit altitude/height, and look carefully for light signals from the ATSU.

The ground to air light signals are:

Light Signal	To an aircraft in flight
Steady green	Cleared to land
Steady red	Give way to other aircraft and continue circling
Series of green flashes	Return for landing (*)
Series of red flashes	Aerodrome unsafe, do not land
Series of white flashes	Land at this aerodrome and proceed to apron (*)
(*) Clearances to land and to taxi will be given in due course.	

Figure C5.2
Light signals from an ATSU to an aircraft in flight.

Light signals can also be made to an aircraft (or vehicle) on the ground:

Light Signal	To an aircraft on the ground
Steady green	Cleared for take-off
Steady red	Stop
Series of green flashes	Cleared to taxi
Series of red flashes	Taxi clear of landing area in use
Series of white flashes	Return to starting point on the aerodrome

Figure C5.3
Light signals from an ATSU to an aircraft or vehicle on the ground.

An aircraft can make the following non-radio signals:

Aircraft in flight		
Message	Signal	Notes
I acknowledge your light signal	Rock aircraft's wings	Daylight only, not used on base leg or final approach
I acknowledge your light signal	Flashing on and off the aircraft's landing lights twice or, if not equipped, switching on and off navigation lights twice	Night-time only

Aircraft on ground		
Message	Signal	Notes
I acknowledge your light signal	Moving the aircraft's ailerons or rudder	Daylight only
I acknowledge your light signal	Flashing on and off the aircraft's landing lights twice or, if not equipped, switching on and off navigation lights twice	Night-time only

Figure C5.4
Non-radio signals from an aircraft to an ATSU.

Occasionally, an aircraft may suffer communications problems which are not a full radio failure, but which make communications more difficult. In these circumstances, there are some standard phraseology words which can be useful:

Word / Phrase	Meaning
HOW DO YOU READ?	What is the readability of my transmission?
I SAY AGAIN	I repeat for emphasis or clarity
SAY AGAIN	Repeat all, or a specified part, of your last transmission
SPEAK SLOWER	Reduce your rate of speech
WORDS TWICE	(As a request): Communication is difficult, transmit every word, or group of words, twice
	(As information): Because communications are difficult, every word, or group of words, in this message will be transmitted twice

Figure C5.5
Standard phraseology when communications are difficult.

These phrases can also be used in the course of normal radio conversation to avoid confusion or uncertainty, in other words:

If in doubt, shout

Progress check

40. What is a 'blind transmission'
41. In the Speechless Code, what is the code for 'request a homing (to the airfield)'?
42. What light signal from an ATSU to an aircraft in flight means 'cleared to land'?
43. What is the meaning of the light signal of red flashes directed at an aircraft of the ground?
44. What visual signal can an aircraft in flight make to acknowledge a light signal by daylight?
45. What phrase can be used to request the sender to repeat all, or a specified part, of his/her last transmission?

These questions are intended to test knowledge and reinforce some of the key learning points from this section. In answering these questions, a 'pass rate' of about 80% should be the target.

Model answers are found at page C94

C6 Distress and Urgency Procedures

Emergency frequencies and facilities

Distress procedures

Urgency procedures

Progress check

"PAN PAN, PAN PAN, PAN PAN

N *Bristol approach...*

A *G-DASH, Rockwell Commander...*

N *with a rough-running engine...*

I *diverting to Bristol airfield...*

P *position one mile west abeam Clevedon*

A *FL50, heading 160...*

three POB."

Distress and Urgency Procedures

Emergency frequencies and facilities

The Standardised Rules of the air (SERA) are very clear about the responsibilities of the Air Traffic Services in the event that an aircraft has an emergency:

> *"In case of an aircraft known or believed to be in a state of emergency...ATS units shall give the aircraft maximum consideration, assistance and priority over other aircraft, as may be necessitated by the circumstances.*
>
> *Subsequent ATC actions shall be based on the intentions of the pilot, the overall air traffic situation and the real-time dynamics of the contingency."*

This rule is only putting into formal legal language the understanding that all involved in the operation of aircraft already have – namely that if an aircraft has an emergency, every assistance and every facility will be made available to enable a safe outcome. And just to be clear, that assistance applies every bit as much to a single-seat light aircraft as it does to the largest airliner full of passengers.

However, for that assistance to be provided, the Air Traffic Services first have to know that an emergency situation exists.

The usual protocol is that an **emergency message** should be made on the frequency in use. If there is no frequency in use, or if there is no reply on the frequency in use, or if there is some other pressing reason not to use the frequency currently in use, then an emergency call should be made on the VHF emergency frequency of 121.5MHz.

This emergency frequency is monitored by ATSUs all over the world – most often by large 'area control' ATC centres and military ATC units, as well as at many major airports. In addition, aircraft flying over prescribed areas are required to keep a listening watch ('guard') on 121.5MHz. In practice, this provision is adhered to principally by commercial flights and those operating long-over water flights or over other remote areas. However, SERA does stipulate that any flight should 'guard' the emergency frequency if it is practical to do so (which usually requires two communications radios in the aircraft). This network of stations listening out on the emergency frequency means that when a call is made on 121.5MHz in most parts of Europe, there is a very good chance that a number of ground stations and/or airborne aircraft will hear the message and be able to alert the appropriate services.

The facilities available to an aircraft with an emergency are dictated mostly by the nature of the emergency and the pilot's requirements. The pilot of an aircraft that is lost can expect all assistance necessary to be located and steered in the desired direction. The pilot of an aircraft needing to land urgently can expect that almost any airfield will be made available without question. The pilot of an aircraft making a forced landing can expect that surface emergency services and other aircraft will be directed to the location.

If an emergency situation does develop, and the pilot considers that an emergency message is necessary or prudent, the next decision is dictated by how serious the emergency is.

Distress procedures

A **distress** situation is the most serious level of emergency, and means *"a condition of being threatened by serious and/or imminent danger and of requiring immediate assistance."* An aircraft in distress takes priority over all other aircraft, and communications to and from an aircraft in distress take priority over all other radio communications.

An initial distress call should (where possible and appropriate to the circumstances) take the following form:

- The word "*MAYDAY*" repeated three times
- The **NAME** of the ATS station addressed
- The **AIRCRAFT** identification (eg call sign and type)
- The **NATURE** of the emergency
- The **INTENTION** of the pilot-in-command
- The aircraft's **POSITION**
- The aircraft's **ALTITUDE** (or level) and heading

In addition, the message can contain any other useful information as the situation dictates, for example remaining aircraft endurance/fuel, number of persons on board, possible presence of hazardous materials, aircraft colour/markings, survival aids etc.

For those who like mnemonics, this idealised sequence for a distress call can be remembered as 'NAN IPA'. Here is an example of a distress call:

"MAYDAY, MAYDAY, MAYDAY

N   *Southampton approach...*

A   *AUTOAIR 3, Piper Malibu...*

N   *complete engine failure...*

I   *intend forced landing at Beaulieu disused airfield...*

P   *current position one mile north of Lymington*

A   *altitude 1500 feet, heading 340...*

two POB."

(POB = Persons On Board)

This idealised format for an emergency call is required for training and tests, and also a good way of covering all the essential information regarding an emergency. However, in a real-life emergency (when, as always, communications are further down the order of the pilot's priorities than aviating and navigating), you can probably communicate the most important elements of an emergency message by remembering the 'three Ps', namely:

- What is the **Problem**?
- What are you **Planning** to do?
- What is your **Position**?

A pilot hearing a distress message should note down as many details as possible (in case no-one else has heard the call). Distress communications have absolute priority over all other communications and pilots aware of distress communications must not transmit on the frequency concerned unless:

- The distress situation is cancelled;
- The distress traffic is transferred to another frequency;
- The ATS unit controlling communications gives permission;
- The pilot is able to offer assistance.

Nevertheless, a pilot hearing a distress communication should continue listening (and taking notes if relevant) until it is evident that assistance is being provided to the aircraft in distress.

The aircraft in distress, or the ATS unit in control of the distress traffic, can impose silence on all aircraft on frequency, or on any particular aircraft which interferes with the distress traffic. This silence instruction can be addressed 'to all stations' or to one station only, using the words "*Stop transmitting, Mayday*". The ATS unit may transfer all other aircraft to another frequency if appropriate.

An aircraft can cancel the distress situation, and an ATS unit can make a general broadcast to announce that the emergency situation has ended: "*Distress traffic ended*".

If a distress message cannot be made for any reason, Air Traffic Services can also be alerted to an emergency situation by the use of the transponder code 7700. Other ways of indicating a distress situation, arguably less practical than a 'Mayday call' or use of the emergency transponder code, include:

- Sending 'SOS' in morse code (• • •   – – –   • • •);
- Sending a text-based message which includes the word 'Mayday';
- Firing rockets or shells showing red lights;
- A parachute flare showing a red light.

Urgency procedures

An **urgency** situation is a less-severe level of emergency than 'distress'. An urgency situation is defined as "*a condition concerning the safety of an aircraft or other vehicle, or of some person on board or within sight, but which does not require immediate assistance.*"

An aircraft with an urgency situation takes precedence over all other aircraft, except an aircraft in distress. Likewise, communications to and from an aircraft with an urgency situation take precedence over all other radio calls, except those to and from an aircraft in distress.

An initial urgency call should take broadly the same form as a distress message, although prefixed with the spoken words 'PAN PAN'. Thus the form of an urgency message is

- The words "***PAN PAN***" repeated three times
- The **NAME** of the ATS station addressed
- The **AIRCRAFT** identification (eg call sign and type)
- The **NATURE** of the urgency situation
- The **INTENTION** of the pilot-in-command
- The aircraft's **POSITION**
- The aircraft's **ALTITUDE** (or level) and heading

In addition, the message can contain any other useful information as the situation dictates. As a mnemonic, the format of an urgency call can also be remembered as NAN IPA.

Here is an example of an Urgency message:

"PAN PAN, PAN PAN, PAN PAN

N *Bristol approach…*

A *G-DASH, Rockwell Commander…*

N *with a rough-running engine…*

I *diverting to Bristol airfield…*

P *position one mile west abeam Clevedon*

A *FL50, heading 160…*

three POB."

Once again, if this idealised format of an urgency call eludes you in a real emergency, just remember the 'three Ps':

* What is the **Problem**?

* What are you **Planning** to do?

* What is your **Position**?

Urgency communications have priority over all other radio traffic except distress communications, and all ATS units and aircraft must take care not to interfere with transmissions to or from an aircraft with an urgency situation.

Other ways of indicating an urgency situation include:

* Sending 'XXX' in morse code (−••− −••− −••−);

* Sending a text-based message which includes the words 'Pan Pan'.

If an aircraft wishes to give notice of difficulties which compel it to land, but which do not require immediate assistance, other signals the pilot can use are:

* the repeated switching on and off of the landing lights; or

* the repeated switching on and off of the navigation lights in such way not be to confused with flashing navigation lights.

There are other situations which imply that an aircraft requires priority handling over other traffic. The term 'minimum fuel' describes a situation where an aircraft's fuel level has reached a state where the flight is committed to land at a specific aerodrome and no additional delay can be accepted. The pilot should use this term to inform ATC that all planned landing airfield options have been reduced to a single specific aerodrome of intended landing. Moreover, any change to the existing clearance may result in landing with less than planned final reserve fuel. 'Minimum fuel' is not an emergency situation, but an indication that an emergency situation is possible should any additional delay occur.

Progress check

46. What is the VHF Emergency Frequency?

47. How is a 'distress' situation defined?

48. Assume you are flying a Cessna 182 call sign AeroAir 2, in two-way communication with Haworth approach and at an altitude 3000ft, heading 180° two miles south of Hightown, when you suffer an engine failure. You have two passengers. What would be the content of a suitable emergency call?

49. What is a situation 'concerning the safety of the aircraft or other vehicle, or some person on board or within sight, but which does not require immediate assistance', and what words can be used to indicate this situation in a radio message?

50. Assume you are flying a Piper PA28 call sign G-BREW, in two-way communication with Northly Information, at an altitude of 2000 feet, heading 270° and three miles east of the airfield, when the engine begins to run roughly and you decide to route directly to the airfield for landing. You are flying solo. What would be the content of a suitable emergency call?

51. What radio messages do urgency calls have priority over?

These questions are intended to test knowledge and reinforce some of the key learning points from this section. In answering these questions, a 'pass rate' of about 80% should be the target.

Model answers are found at page C94

National Procedures

National rules and procedures

Progress check

National Procedures

National rules and procedures

The following information applies to the United Kingdom (UK), which for the purposes of this publication consists of England, Wales, Scotland and Northern Ireland. It should be noted that some territories that might normally be considered to be part of the UK, such as the Channel Islands and the Isle of Man, have their own aviation legislation. The information in relation to UK rules and procedures is limited to those elements which are significantly different to the European or ICAO procedures described in the main text and is presented under the chapter headings used in sections C1 – C6.

C1 VHF Radio Broadcast

Factors affecting VHF radio range

The UK Aeronautical Information Publication (AIP) gives general advice that radio communications from aircraft to ATSUs should only take place within the following boundaries:

- For international airfields, Approach (APP) frequencies: a radius of 25nm from the airfield, up to a height of 10,000ft.

- For international airfields, Tower (TWR) frequencies: a radius of 25nm from the airfield, up to a height of 4,000ft.

- At other airfields, TWR, AFIS or Air/Ground Communications Service (AGCS – call sign 'radio') frequencies: up to 10nm from the airfield, up to a height of 3,000ft.

- At airfields with no notified specific frequency, when the pilot is using the 'SAFETYCOM' frequency (described shortly), radio transmissions must only be made within a maximum range of 10nm from the aerodrome of intended landing, and below 2000 feet above the aerodrome elevation.

Although the above limitations are given as general advice, for most frequencies listed in the UK AIP a specific 'Designated Operational Coverage' (DOC) is published which can be taken as over-ruling the generalised recommended distance/height limitations. The size of the DOC for a specific frequency is almost invariably greater than the applicable general advice, and is found within the AIP entry for the specific airfield.

Figure C7.0

An extract from the UK AIP showing communication frequencies for Ronaldsway (Isle of Man) airport and the applicable 'Designated Operational Coverage' (DOC) for each frequency.

EGNS AD 2.18 AIR TRAFFIC SERVICES COMMUNICATION FACILITIES

Service Designation	Callsign	Channel(s)	Hours of Operation	Remarks	
1	2	3	4	5	
APP	RONALDSWAY APPROACH	135.900 MHz Also CTR channel. DOC 50 nm/16,000 ft.	Mon-Sat 0600-2045 (0500-1945); Sun 0645-2045 (0545-1945); and by arrangement.	ATZ hours coincident with Approach hours. In the event of failure of remote transmitters/receivers, coverage to the north of the airfield may be degraded and ATC services reduced accordingly.	→▌ →▌
TWR	RONALDSWAY TOWER	119.000 MHz DOC 25 nm/8,000 ft.	Mon-Sat 0600-2045 (0500-1945); Sun 0645-2045 (0545-1945); and by arrangement.		→▌ →▌
RAD	RONALDSWAY RADAR	135.900 MHz DOC 50 nm/16,000 ft.	Mon-Sat 0600-2045 (0500-1945); Sun 0645-2045 (0545-1945).	In the event of failure of remote transmitters/receivers, coverage to the north of the airfield may be degraded and ATC services reduced accordingly.	→▌
	RONALDSWAY RADAR	120.850 MHz As directed by ATC. DOC 50 nm/16,000 ft.	Mon-Sat 0600-2045 (0500-1945); Sun 0645-2045 (0545-1945).		→▌ →▌
	RONALDSWAY RADAR	125.300 MHz As directed by ATC. DOC 25 nm/10,000 ft.	Mon-Sat 0600-2045 (0500-1945); Sun 0645-2045 (0545-1945).		→▌

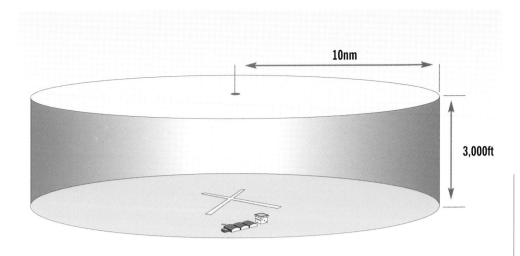

Figure C7.1
On the 'Tower' frequency at non-international airfields, plus all AFIS and AGCS units, the UK CAA recommend that radio communications should be limited to aircraft below 3000ft and within 10nm of the airfield.

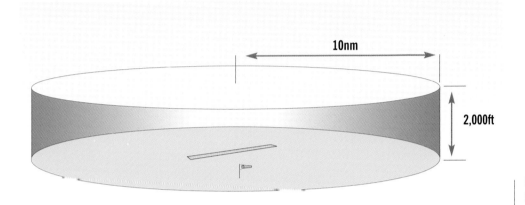

Figure C7.2
When using the 'Safetycom' frequency, the UK CAA recommend that radio communications should be limited to below 2000ft above the airfield and within 10nm of the airfield.

C2 Transmission Technique

Transmission of numbers

When transmitting numbers representing Flight Levels which are whole 'hundreds', the UK CAA specifies that the term 'hundred' be used:

Level	Transmitted as (UK)
FL100	Flight Level One Hundred
FL200	Flight Level Two Hundred
FL300	Flight Level Three Hundred

Figure C7.3
UK procedure for transmitting flight levels.

When referring to a pressure setting which is below 1000 hectopascals, the word "*hectopascal*" should be included after the pressure setting.

Call signs

In the UK, student pilots who do not yet hold a licence and who are flying solo as part of their training must prefix the aircraft call sign with the word "**student**" on an initial call to an ATSU. The ATSU will acknowledge this prefix, but then it does not need to be used again unless the student pilot changes frequency. The ATSU will, as far as is practicable, make allowance for the limited experience and ability of student pilots in their communications and in particular the complexity of instructions and/or information passed to the student.

UK Air Traffic Control uses the following call signs, in addition to those recognised in SERA:

ATC service	Call Sign Suffix
Military traffic zone crossing service	Zone
Approach control radar arrivals	Director / Arrivals
Precision Approach Radar	Talkdown
Ground movement planning, clearance delivery	Delivery

Figure C7.4
UK-specific Air Traffic Control call signs.

Bristol	ATIS 126.025	TWR 133.850	DIR 136.075	DEL 121.925	FIRE 121.600	Listening Squawk 5077 125.650

Figure C7.5
ATC frequencies and call signs in a commercial flight guide.

C3 VFR Communications Procedures

Standard phraseology
In addition to the standard phraseology already listed, the UK also permits the use of the following phraseology.

Word/Phrase	Meaning	Notes
CHANGING TO	I intend to call [unit] on [frequency]	
CONTACT	Establish communications with [ATSU] – your details have been passed to them	This is slightly different to the ICAO/EASA definition of this word
CONTINUE WITH	Used when it is known that an aircraft has already established contact with another unit, or when details have been passed to the next unit but no radar handover has taken place.	
CORRECTION	An error has been made in this transmission (or the message indicated). The correct version is....	
FANSTOP	I am initiating a practice engine failure after take-off	Used only by pilots of single engine aircraft. The response from the ATSU should be "Report climbing away".
FREECALL	Call [ATSU] – your details have not been passed to them	Used mostly by military units
HOLD SHORT	Stop before reaching the specified location	Only used in limited circumstances where no defined point exists, or to emphasis a clearance limit
SQUAWK EMERGENCY or SQUAWK 7700	Select the emergency transponder code (7700)	

Figure C7.6
UK-specific standard phraseology.

The official source of information on radio communications frequencies, call signs, services etc. is the **UK Aeronautical Information Publication (AIP)**. Airfield frequencies for a 'licenced' airfield are mostly found in the 'AD' (Aerodrome) section of the AIP under the specific airfield entry. Information on radio frequencies at 'unlicenced' airfields (such as private air strips) is found in commercial flight guides or by contacting the airfield directly before flight.

'En-route' communications services and radio frequencies are found in the 'ENR' (En-Route) section of the AIP. Radio frequencies for UK military airfields are also found in the ENR section.

In the UK, ATC clearances are issued solely for the purposes of expediting and separating air traffic and are based on known traffic conditions which affect safety in aircraft operations. If an air traffic control clearance is not suitable to the pilot-in-command of an aircraft, the flight crew may request and, if practicable, obtain an amended clearance. Air traffic control clearances issued by Air Traffic Control units are authority for an aircraft to proceed so far as known air traffic is concerned. ATC clearances are not authority to violate any applicable regulations; neither do clearances relieve a pilot-in-command of any responsibility at all in connection with the violation of applicable rules and regulations.

Occasionally, instances of false or deceptive transmissions on ATC frequencies can occur. Pilots should challenge or verify with the ATC unit concerned any instruction or clearance issued to them which they regard as suspect. In other words:

If in doubt; shout

In UK airspace, **Flight Information Service (FIS)** can be provided in a number of different forms, principally for aircraft flying outside controlled airspace – although these services are also available to aircraft flying VFR in Class E airspace. These types of FIS (**Basic, Traffic, Deconfliction and Procedural**) are sometimes referred to under the general heading of Air Traffic Services Outside Controlled Airspace (ATSOCAS).

Within Class G (uncontrolled) airspace, regardless of the service being provided, pilots are ultimately responsible for collision avoidance and terrain clearance. It is the pilot's responsibility to determine the appropriate service for the various phases and conditions of flight and request that service from the Air Traffic Controller or Flight Information Service Officer (FISO). The Deconfliction and Procedural Services are only provided to flights operating under Instrument Flight Rules (IFR), which is outside the scope of this book and so these services are not considered further.

In the UK, an aircraft receiving some form of Flight Information Service (or an Air Traffic Control Service) is also, by default, receiving an Alerting Service.

Instructions issued by controllers or FISOs to pilots operating outside controlled airspace are not mandatory; however, the services rely upon pilot compliance with the specified terms and conditions. Agreements can be established between a controller and a pilot for the operation of the aircraft to be restricted laterally or vertically. Except for safety reasons, a pilot must not deviate from an agreement without first advising, and obtaining a response from, the controller.

A **Basic Service** provides advice and information which may include weather information, changes of serviceability of facilities, conditions at aerodromes, general airspace activity information, and any other information likely to affect safety. Avoiding other traffic is solely the pilot's responsibility. Pilots should not expect any form of traffic information from a controller/FISO when operating under a Basic Service and the pilot remains responsible for collision avoidance at all times. However, a controller/FISO can provide traffic information in general terms to assist with the pilot's situational awareness. This will not normally be updated by the controller/FISO. A Basic Service is available at all levels and the pilot remains responsible for terrain clearance at all times. Unless the pilot has entered into an agreement with a controller to maintain a specific course of action, a pilot may change heading, route, or level without advising the controller. A controller will not issue specific heading instructions; however, general navigational assistance may be provided on request.

A **Traffic Service** is a surveillance-based (eg radar) air traffic service, where in addition to the provisions of a Basic Service, the controller provides specific surveillance-derived traffic information to assist the pilot in avoiding other traffic. Nevertheless, ultimately the avoidance of other traffic is solely the pilot's responsibility. If a controller issues a heading and/or level that would require flight in Instrument Meteorological Conditions (IMC), a pilot who is not suitably qualified to fly in IMC must inform the controller and request alternative instructions. The controller will pass traffic information on relevant traffic, and update the traffic information if it constitutes a hazard, or if requested by the pilot. However, high controller workload and radio frequency loading may reduce the ability of the controller to pass traffic information, and keep such information up-to-date. Whether traffic information has been passed or not, the pilot is responsible for collision avoidance without assistance from the controller. Subject to surveillance system coverage, a Traffic Service may be provided at any level; the pilot remains responsible for terrain clearance at all times.

When receiving a Traffic Service, a pilot may operate under their own navigation or a controller may provide headings and levels for the purpose of positioning, sequencing or as navigational assistance. If a heading or level is unacceptable to the pilot they must advise the controller immediately. When operating under their own navigation, pilots may alter course as required; however, unless safety is likely to be compromised, pilots shall not change their general route or manoeuvring area without first advising and obtaining a response from the controller. When following an ATC heading, or flying at a level allocated by ATC, a pilot must not change heading, level or level band without first advising ATC and obtaining a response from the controller, unless safety is likely to be compromised.

A pilot may choose to make a request for a particular service in the initial call to an ATSU:

 "Newcastle Approach, Avstar 908,
*request **Basic Service**"*

The agreement between controller/FISO and pilot regarding the type of air traffic service being provided is one of the items that needs to be read-back:

 *"Condor 32, **Traffic Service**"*

 *"**Traffic Service**, Condor 32"*

Inside UK Class B, C and D controlled airspace, a VFR or Special VFR flight is likely to be provided with a **Radar Control Service**. As the name implies, this is an Air Traffic Control service based on radar identification of the aircraft. If an aircraft is entering controlled airspace, it is likely that it will be offered a 'basic' or 'traffic' service whilst outside controlled airspace, changing to a Radar Control Service when the aircraft enters controlled airspace. When a flight is receiving a Radar Control Service, the pilot is assumed to be complying with the controller's instructions, unless the pilot advises otherwise.

If traffic avoidance advice is issued on request to a VFR or Special VFR flight under a Radar Control Service, the controller is not required to maintain any specific minimum distance between a VFR/SVFR flight and other traffic. Any 'avoiding action' instructions are aimed at reducing the risk of getting too close to other aircraft, but the pilot of a VFR or Special VFR flight is ultimately responsible for maintaining a safe separation from other traffic.

The call sign 'radio' in relation to a UK ATSU is used to identify an aerodrome **Air/Ground Communication Service (AGCS)**. An AGCS can be provided by Radio Operators who are not licensed but have obtained a certificate of competency from the UK CAA to operate radio equipment. The operation of an AGCS is not regulated in any other way, AGCS is not regarded by the UK CAA as an Air Traffic Service, because it does not include an alerting service.

AGCS operators may provide traffic and weather information to pilots operating at and in the vicinity of the aerodrome. Any traffic information is based primarily on reports made by other pilots. Information provided by an AGCS radio station operator may be used to assist a pilot in making a decision; however, the CAA stress that the safe conduct of the flight remains the pilot's responsibility.

Climb/descent clearances: in the UK, when giving a clearance or instruction to climb or descent to a Flight level, the word 'To' is omitted. For example:

 *"G-OR, **climb** flight level 60"*

All messages relating to a climb or descent in relation to an 'Altitude' or 'Height' must include the word 'to', followed immediately by the word 'Altitude' or 'Height' as appropriate:

 *"Rainair 45, **climb to altitude 3500 feet, QHN 1024**"*

 *"Cessna UW, **descend to height 1700 feet, QFE 1007**"*

Traffic Information terminology: Whenever practicable, a UK ATSU will give traffic information in the following form:

- The relative bearing of the conflicting traffic in terms of the 12 hour clock with the optional prefix 'left or right' as appropriate; or, if the aircraft under service is established in a turn, the relative position of the conflicting traffic in relation to cardinal points ie northwest, south etc.;

- The distance from the conflicting traffic;

- The relative movement of the conflicting traffic; or, if the aircraft under service is established in a turn, the direction of flight of the conflicting traffic in relation to cardinal points;

- The level of aircraft, if known;

- The speed of the conflicting traffic, if relevant; and

- The type of aircraft, if relevant.

Relative movement will be described by using one of the following terms as applicable:

Crossing, including either 'left to right' or 'right to left', where there is change in the relative bearing between the conflicting traffic's flight path and that of the aircraft under service. Controllers should include the words 'ahead' or 'behind'.

Converging, where there appears to be no change in relative bearing between the conflicting traffic's flight path and that of the aircraft under service and/or the controller believes that there is a significant risk of mid-air collision.

Same direction where the conflicting traffic's flight path is the same as that of the aircraft under service.

Opposite direction where the conflicting traffic's flight path is approximately 180° opposed to that of the aircraft under service but the flight paths are not converging.

Manoeuvring where the conflicting traffic's flight path and/or level information is unpredictable and/or showing significant variation.

The level of conflicting traffic will be given using one of the following terms:

Same Level;

[number of] **feet above/below**;

[number of] **feet above/below cleared level**;

indicating [number of] **feet above/below**;

indicating same level;

indicating [number of] **feet above/below cleared level**;

at [level]**;**

indicating [level]; or

no height information

The speed of conflicting traffic may be described as **fast moving** or **slow moving**.

Having been given traffic information, pilots can acknowledge in one of two ways: *"Traffic in sight"* or *"Traffic not sighted"*.

Figure C7.6a

Details of the UK Lower Airspace Radar Service (LARS) are found in the UK AIP and commercial flight guides.

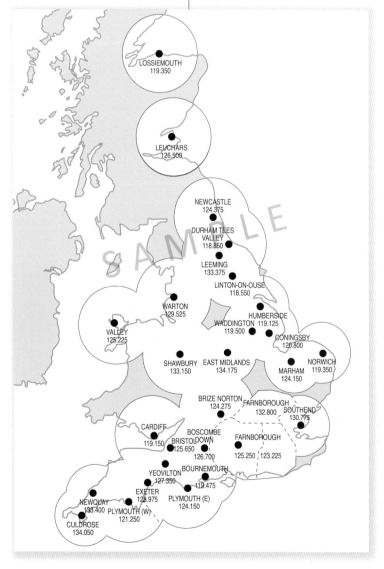

In the UK a network of ATC radar units provide the UK **Lower Airspace Radar Service** (**LARS**). LARS is available to all aircraft flying outside Controlled Airspace up to FL 100, within the limits of radar/radio cover. The service will be provided within approximately 30nm of each participating Unit and unless the Unit is active 24 hours a day (H24), LARS will normally be available from Mondays to Fridays between 0800 and 1700 UTC in the Winter, 0700 and 1600 UTC in the Summer. As some participating units may stay open to cover evening, night or weekend flying, pilots are recommended to call for the service even outside the published hours of ATS. If no reply is received after three consecutive calls, it should be assumed that the service is not available. LARS will not normally be available from non-H24 Units at weekends and during public holidays. The coverage of many LARS units 'overlaps' and often a LARS unit can arrange an automatic 'handover' to the next unit on the aircraft's route, which can help reduce pilot workload.

Full details of the UK LARS network are found in the UK AIP.

The Visual Circuit: if an arriving aircraft is instructed or requested to make a **Standard Overhead Join** at a UK airfield, the following procedure should be applied:

- Overfly the airfield at 2000ft above airfield level;

- Descend on the 'dead side' to circuit height/altitude;

- Join the circuit by crossing the upwind end of the runway at circuit height/altitude;

- Position downwind.

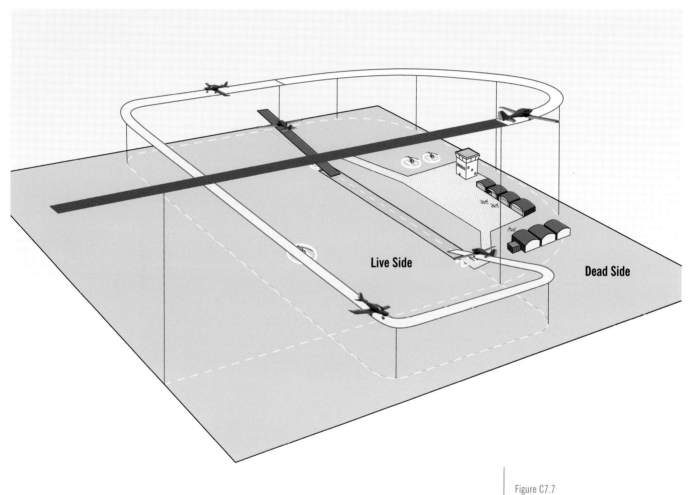

Figure C7.7
The UK Standard Overhead Join.

At some airfields the overflying height may be modified from the above, and as a matter of general protocol, most pilots expect that an aircraft making a Standard Overhead Join will make all turns in the same direction as the circuit (eg if the circuit is left-hand, make all turns to the left).

In the visual circuit itself, the following key positions are recognised in the UK:

- **Downwind** – Pilots are to report 'Downwind' when abeam the upwind end of the runway. Pilots should report '**Late downwind**' if, on downwind leg, they have been unable to report 'Downwind' and have passed abeam the downwind end of the runway.

- **Base Leg** – Pilots are to report 'Base', if requested to do so, immediately on completing the turn on to base leg.

- **Final** – Pilots are to report 'Final' after completing the turn on to final approach and when at a range of not more than 4nm from the approach end of the runway (or 'Long Final' if between 8nm and 4nm from the runway).

Figure C7.8

Main reporting point in the UK visual circuit.

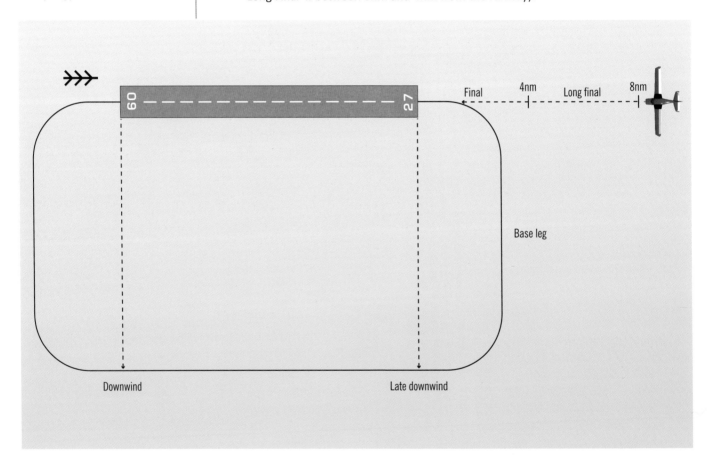

Land after procedure: under the Air Navigation Order (ANO), in the UK aircraft must not land on a runway if there is already another aircraft on the runway, unless an air traffic control unit at the airfield authorises an aircraft to **land after**. When an ATC unit chooses to permit a 'land after' – that is an aircraft allowed to land on a runway before another landing aircraft ahead has cleared the runway – the following restrictions apply:

- The runway must be long enough to complete the 'land after' safely;
- The landings must take place during daylight hours;
- The second landing aircraft must be able to see the first aircraft clearly and continuously until it is clear of the runway;
- The second landing aircraft must have been warned.

ATC will provide this warning by issuing the second landing aircraft with the instruction "***Land after** [first aircraft type]*".

Responsibility for ensuring safe separation between the two aircraft remains with the pilot of the second landing aircraft.

Figure C7.9
In the UK an ATC unit may authorise an aircraft to 'land after' another aircraft which is still on the runway.

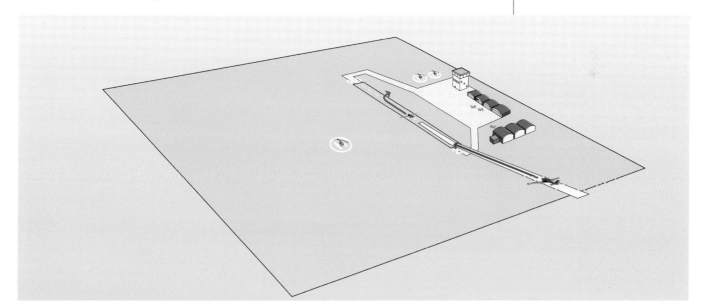

Aerodrome Flight Information Service (AFIS): in the UK, an AFIS unit is permitted to issue taxi instructions to aircraft on the apron and manoeuvring area, in addition to *"...information useful for the safe and efficient conduct of aerodrome traffic"*. In the UK, an AFIS can only be provided by a qualified Aerodrome Flight Information Service Officer (AFISO). An AFISO is responsible for:

- Issuing information to aircraft flying in and in the vicinity of the Aerodrome Traffic Zone (ATZ) to assist pilots in preventing collisions;
- Issuing instructions and information to aircraft on the apron and manoeuvring area to assist pilots in preventing collisions between aircraft and vehicles/obstructions on the manoeuvring area, or between aircraft moving on the apron;
- Issuing instructions to vehicles and persons on the manoeuvring area;
- Informing aircraft of essential aerodrome information (ie the state of the aerodrome and its facilities);
- Provision of an alerting service;
- Initiating overdue action.

A UK AFIS unit also uses slightly different terminology in relation to aircraft taking-off and landing, for example:

 "Broughton Information, G-RHMS request taxi"

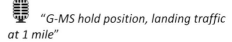 *"G-MS, Broughton Information. Runway 32 wind 300 13 knots, QNH 999 hectopascals. Taxi holding point A2 via taxiway C"*

 "Runway 32 QNH 999 hectopascals, taxi holding point A2 via taxiway C, G-MS"

 "Ready for departure, G-MS"

 "G-MS hold position, landing traffic at 1 mile"

 "Holding, G-MS"

 *"G-MS, surface wind 290 10 knots, runway 32 **take-off at your discretion**"*

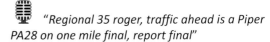 *"Runway 32 taking off, G-MS"*

 "Regional 35, downwind"

"Regional 35 roger, traffic ahead is a Piper PA28 on one mile final, report final"

 "Traffic in sight, wilco, Regional 35"

"Regional 35, Final"

*"Regional 35, surface wind 200 14 knots, runway 24 **land at your discretion**"*

 "Regional 35, roger, runway 24 landing"

Air Ground Communication Service (**AGCS**): an AGCS operator must be especially careful not to make any transmission that could be mistaken for a clearance or instruction, nor be misinterpreted as coming from an AFIS unit. Here is a typical departure and arrival sequence at an airfield with an AGCS (and so using the call sign suffix 'radio').

"Westray radio, G-TIPS request airfield and taxi information"

"G-PS runway 15 wind 120 15 knots, QNH 1017"

"Runway 15, QNH 1017, G-PS"

"G-PS, ready for departure"

*"G-PS **no reported traffic**, surface wind 100 20 knots*

"Roger, taking off, G-PS"

"Unst radio, G-SAMZ"

"G-SAMZ, Unst radio, pass your message"

"G-SAMZ, Cessna 150, 5 miles south of the airfield at 1800 feet, for landing"

"G-MS, runway 12 left hand, QNH 1001, no reported traffic"

"Runway 12 left hand, QNH 1001 G-MS"

"Downwind, G-MS"

"G-MS, one Cessna 172 lining-up runway 12"

"Traffic in sight, G-MS"

"Final, G-MS"

"G-MS, Cessna has just departed runway 12"

"Roger, landing, G-MS"

C75

SAFETYCOM: where a UK airfield does not have a notified radio frequency, a common frequency called **SAFETYCOM** is available, pilots may use this frequency to broadcast their intentions for safety purposes.

SAFETYCOM can only be used at airfields which do not have a notified radio frequency. If a VHF frequency is published for an airfield, that frequency must be used, even outside the notified operating hours. Transmissions on the SAFETYCOM frequency should only be made within 10nm of the airfield of intended landing, and not above 2000 feet above the airfield elevation (or not more than 1000ft above the published circuit height/altitude). SAFETYCOM must only be used to transmit the pilot's intentions, and no response should be expected, except where another pilot also needs to transmit his or her intentions.

It cannot be assumed that all other flights in the vicinity are monitoring the frequency and, as at all other times, pilots must maintain a good lookout – no air traffic service is associated with SAFETYCOM. Information transmitted on SAFETYCOM confers no priority or right of way and pilots must comply with the SERA and UK 'Rules of the Air', including the provisions in relation to avoiding collisions.

SAFETYCOM broadcasts may be taking place around a number of airfields at the same time, so it is not uncommon to hear a number of broadcasts relating to different airfields on the SAFETYCOM frequency at the same time. Therefore it is important to use the airfield's name in all transmissions, followed by the suffix 'traffic'.

The SAFETYCOM frequency is published in the UK AIP and commercial flight guides, and at the time of writing it is 135.475MHz.

The phraseology for SAFETYCOM can also be used at 'unattended' airfields when operating outside the notified hours of operation of the ATSU, using the relevant ATSU frequency.

Here are some examples of SAFETYCOM broadcasts:

"Glendoe traffic, G-UNGO lining up for departure runway 04, Glendoe"

"Spanhoe traffic, G-DRAT 5 miles to the south, to join overhead, Spanhoe"

"Spanhoe traffic, G-DRAT overhead, joining for runway 09, Spanhoe"

"Spanhoe traffic, G-DRAT descending deadside runway 09, Spanhoe"

"Spanhoe traffic, G-DRAT downwind runway 09, Spanhoe"

"Spanhoe traffic, G-DRAT final runway 09, Spanhoe"

Military aerodromes: within the UK, active military airfields are usually surrounded by a Military Aerodrome Traffic Zone – MATZ. A MATZ does not have a specific airspace classification, and most MATZ are located in Class G (uncontrolled) airspace, nevertheless, pilots are strongly advised to make contact with a MATZ controlled before entering a MATZ and to comply with the MATZ controller's instructions. Full details of UK MATZ are found in the UK AIP, and an aircraft planning to enter a MATZ is advised to establish contact on the appropriate frequency not less than 15nm distance or 5 minutes flying time from the MATZ boundary (whichever is sooner), and request 'MATZ penetration' in the initial call, for example:

 "Wattisham approach, G-DRGL request MATZ penetration"

Whilst in contact with a MATZ unit, pilots are expected to comply with any instructions issued by controllers (unless the pilot indicates otherwise) and maintain a listening watch on the frequency. Nevertheless, pilots should assume that they remain ultimately responsible for collision avoidance. Pilots should not change heading or level without giving prior notification to the controller and should advise when leaving the MATZ.

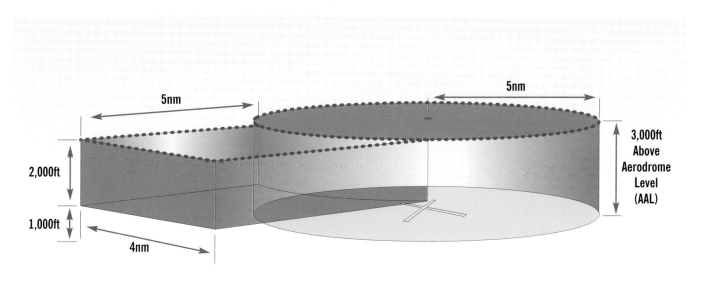

Figure C7.9a
The dimensions of a standard UK Military Aerodrome Traffic Zone – MATZ.

Although the MATZ penetration service may not be available 'H24' (eg 24 hours a day, 7 days a week), the Aerodrome Traffic Zone (ATZ) at almost all military airfields is notified as active at all times and contact must be established before entering an ATZ at a military airfield during its notified hours of operation. Even outside the notified hours of operation of a MATZ or military ATZ, all pilots are strongly advised to attempt to make contact on the notified frequencies and should be aware that non-notified activities may take place on and around military airfields, even outside their notified hours.

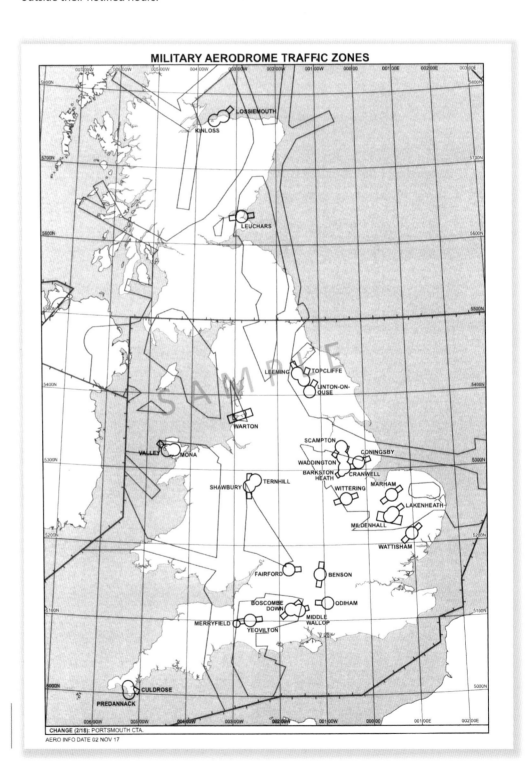

Figure C7.10

A map of Military Aerodrome Traffic Zones (MATZ) in the UK AIP.

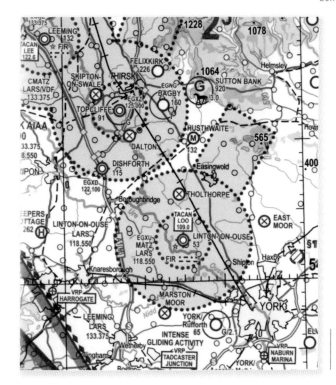

Figure C7.10a

A Military Aerodrome Traffic Zone (MATZ) as depicted on a VFR aeronautical chart.

Mar 2018

ENR 2.2 OTHER REGULATED AIRSPACE (continued)

Note 13: *Civilian traffic joining Wittering will be given Wittering Tower freq 127.975 MHz. On no account free-call Wittering Tower for zone crossing service.*

MATZ	Mid-point of the Longest Runway	AD Elevation (ft)	Stub Heading(s) °T to AD	Controlling Aerodrome	Frequency to be used (MHz)	Remarks
1	2	3	4	5	6	7
Barkston Heath	525746.74N 0003337.16W	367	068 (2 nm stub)	Cranwell	124.450	MATZ 3 nm radius. Stub extends from SFC to 3000 ft aal.
Benson	513654.14N 0010545.05W	203	008/188	Benson	120.900	
Boscombe Down	510911N 0014504W	407	230/050	Boscombe Down	126.700	Note 9.
Coningsby	530535N 0000958W	24	252	Coningsby	119.200	
Cranwell	530147.04N 0002933.91W	218	263	Cranwell	124.450	
Culdrose	500507.43N 0051514.66W	267	293	Culdrose	134.050	
Fairford	514101N 0014725W	286	268	Brize Norton	119.000	Note 1.
Kinloss	573858N 0033338W	22	—	Lossiemouth	119.575	Note 11.
Lakenheath	522433N 000334UE	32	056/236	Lakenheath	128.900	Notes 2 and 3.

Figure C7.10b

Details of UK MATZ will be found in the UK Aeronautical Information Publication (AIP).

UK military airfields may use different terminology to that used at civilian airfields, especially around the visual circuit. The visual circuit at a military airfield also tends to be oval or racetrack in shape, rather than the rectangular circuit shape traditionally used in civilian flying.

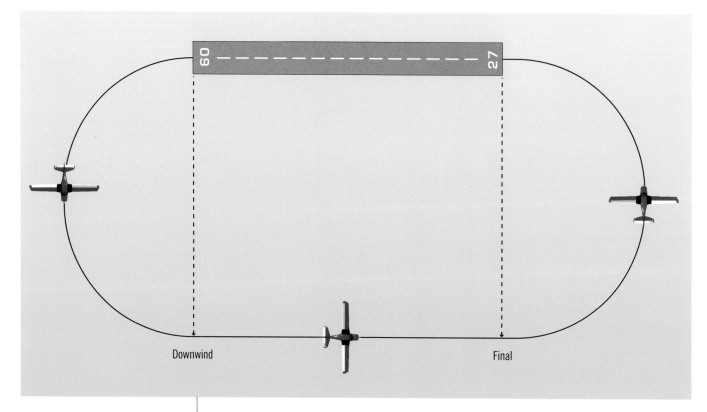

Figure C7.11

The standard position reports in a UK military visual circuit.

Note that in the military circuit, aircraft tend to report 'Final' just before turning onto base leg.

Military controllers may refer to the number of aircraft in the circuit using the phraseology 'Two in' (for two aircraft in the circuit); 'Three in' (for three aircraft in the circuit); etc. Occasionally, a 'touch and go' landing and take-off maybe referred to as a 'roller'. Controllers at military aerodromes may omit the runway designator for take-off, landing, low approach and touch and go clearances where no potential for misunderstanding exists.

Military aircraft often join the visual circuit by flying down the final approach track at circuit height and relatively high speed, from overhead the runway they then make a continuous turn onto the downwind leg whilst slowing down. This procedure is known as a 'run and break' or 'run-in and break'. A military airfield may have an 'initial point' from which the circuit is joined. Once an aircraft has made a run-in and break, it may report 'on the break', which is broadly equivalent to the civilian 'downwind' call.

As part of the 'final' call, pilots of aircraft with retractable undercarriage are expected to state that the undercarriage is down, for example:

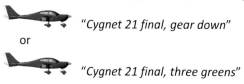

"Cygnet 21 final, gear down"

or

"Cygnet 21 final, three greens"

If the pilot does not make this call at a military aerodrome, the controller may well prompt for confirmation:

 "Cygnet 21 final"

 "Cygnet 21 check gear down"

 "Cygnet 21 gear down"

 "Cygnet 21 cleared to land"

At a military airfield, a controller may clear an aircraft to land if the runway is occupied, by passing information on that traffic, for example:

"Cygnet 21 cleared to land, traffic is a Grob vacating at the end of the runway"

If the runway is occupied by an aircraft performing a 'touch and go', the controller may refer to that aircraft as 'ahead' if it has begun the acceleration phase of the touch and go:

"Cygnet 21 cleared touch and go, one ahead, Grob"

The following words and phrases have specific meanings to UK military controllers:

Word/phrase	Military meaning
CONTINUE WITH	Your details are known to the next controller, but no radar hand over has taken place
CONTACT	A radar handover to the next controller has taken place
FREECALL	It has not been possible to pass your details to the next controller, expect to have to pass the next controller all your flight details
BLOCK	Indicates an aircraft wishes to operate within a vertical block of airspace, the lower and upper limits are usually defined as flight levels

Figure C7.12
UK Military standard phraseology.

VHF Direction Finding

A dwindling number of UK airfields are able to offer a VHF Direction Finding (VDF) service, in which the controller can take a bearing on an aircraft's radio transmission and pass that information to the pilot.

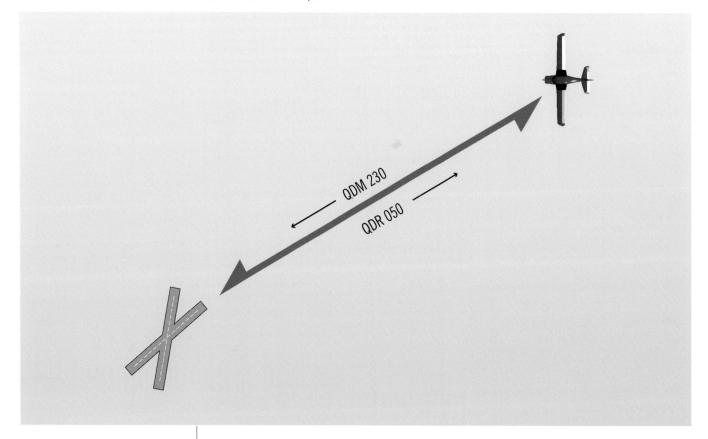

Figure C7.13

A QDM is a bearing **TO** a station, a QDR or 'radial' is a bearing **FROM** a station.

A VDF bearing can be defined in a number of ways, using the 'Q' code:

Q Code	Meaning
QDM	The magnetic track of the aircraft to the VDF station, in other words the magnetic heading to steer to reach the VDF station if there was nil wind
QDR	The magnetic bearing of the aircraft from the VDF station
QTE	The true bearing of the aircraft from the VDF station

The accuracy of a bearing can be classified as below:

Bearing code	Accuracy
Class A	Accurate to with +/- 2°
Class B	Accurate to with +/- 5°
Class C	Accurate to with +/- 10°
Class D	Worse than Class C accuracy

The most obvious use of VDF information by a pilot is to obtain a track to the VDF station. This request is done using the format '[call sign], request QDM, [call sign]'. When the unit passes VDF information to the pilot, it is an item of information requiring read back and each aircraft transmission with VDF information must end with the aircraft's call sign.

"Shoreham Approach, G-KIRB,
***request QDM**, G-KIRB"*

"G-KIRB, Shoreham Approach,
***QDM 130 degrees class Bravo**"*

 *"**QDM 130 degrees class Bravo**,*
G-KIRB"

If the pilot wants to track towards the VDF station, it will be necessary to periodically request a new QDM to check if the aircraft is maintaining a constant track towards the VDF station.

Full details of ATSUs offering a VDF service are found in the UK AIP.

Service Designation	Callsign	Channel(s)	Hours of Operation	Remarks
1	2	3	4	5
APP	WESTLAND AP-PROACH	130.800 MHz DOC 25 nm/6000 ft.	Mon-Thu 0900-1630 (0800-1530), Fri 0900-1530 (0800-1430); except PH.	ATZ hours coincident with Approach hours. VDF 505628.35N 0023943.70W
TWR	WESTLAND TOWER	125.400 MHz DOC 25 nm/4000 ft.	Mon-Thu 0900-1630 (0800-1530), Fri 0900-1530 (0800-1430); except PH.	VDF 505628.35N 0023943.70W

Figure C7.14

An extract from the UK AIP showing the VDF service available at Yeovil airfield.

Radio Mandatory Zones: A **Radio Mandatory Zone (RMZ)** may be established in UK airspace, within which the pilot must maintain continuous two-way communication on the designated frequency. Before entering an RMZ, the pilot must make an initial call stating:

- the designation of the station being called;
- aircraft call sign;
- type of aircraft;
- position;
- level;
- the intentions of the pilot; and,
- Any other information as prescribed by the competent authority

Designation and lateral limits	Vertical Limits	Airspace Class	ATS unit callsign/ language	Transition Altitude	Remarks
1	2	3	4	5	6
HAWARDEN RMZ 1 531309N 0025059W - 530940N 0025059W - 531427N 0030140W - 531309N 0025059W	Upper limit: 2500 ft ALT Lower limit: SFC	G	HAWARDEN RADAR English	5000 ft	RMZ hours coincident with aerodrome hours as detailed at EGNR AD 2.3. For conditions of RMZ entry see EGNR AD 2.22 Flight Procedures. Contiguous with overlying CAS.
HAWARDEN RMZ 2 530940N 0025059W - 530823N 0025059W - 530400N 0025720W - 530845N 0031227W - 531525N 0030250W - 531427N 0030140W - 530940N 0025059W	Upper limit: 3000 ft ALT Lower limit: SFC	G	HAWARDEN RADAR English	5000 ft	Contiguous with overlying CAS.
HAWARDEN RMZ 3 530400N 0025720W - 530000N 0030305W - 530000N 0030711W - 530321N 0031150W - 530845N 0031227W - 530400N 0025720W	Upper limit: 4500 ft ALT Lower limit: SFC	G	HAWARDEN RADAR English	5000 ft	Contiguous with overlying CAS.
HAWARDEN ATZ A circle, 2.5 nm radius centred at 531041N 0025840W on longest notified runway (04/22)	Upper limit: 2000 ft Lower limit: SFC	G	HAWARDEN RADAR English	5000 ft	

Figure C7.15

Details of a Radio Mandatory Zone (RMZ) in the UK AIP.

The UK CAA further require that before entering an RMZ, this call must be acknowledged by ATC. If the call is not acknowledged, or if the pilot is instructed to 'standby' before passing the information, the aircraft must remain outside the RMZ until acknowledgment by ATC is forthcoming.

Helicopter phraseology: In the UK, some **helicopter-specific phraseology** is used. The type of aircraft category (eg helicopter or gyroplane) may be used as a prefix to the call sign, for example "*Helicopter BN*". Helicopter carrying out a Helicopter Emergency Medical Service (HEMS) will often use the call sign prefix 'HELIMED', and are usually given priority over other flights. Helicopters involved in Search And Rescue (SAR) operations often use the call sign prefix 'Rescue Helicopter'.

Figure C7.16
Certain specific items of phraseology apply to helicopters in the UK.

The following phrases may be used in relation to helicopters:

Phrase	Meaning/Notes
Air-Taxi	Used in place of 'taxi', the helicopter is expected to proceed at a slow speed above the surface, normally below 20 knots and in ground effect
Cleared to land [location]	Used to authorise a helicopter to land at a specific location on the manoeuvring area. At an 'AFIS' airfield, the phrase 'Land at your discretion [location]' may be used
Cleared to take-off [location]	Used to authorise a helicopter to take-off at a specific location on the manoeuvring area. At an 'AFIS' airfield, the phrase 'Take-off at your discretion [location]' may be used
Ground Taxi	Used to indicate the movement of a helicopter on the surface, under its own power. This could be required for a helicopter which is fitted with wheels, to reduce rotor downwash
Hold	If an air-taxiing helicopter is instructed to 'hold', it is free to hover or touch down at the pilot's discretion
Hold in the hover	The air taxiing helicopter is to hold position without touching down
Hover	Hold position whilst hovering in ground effect, waiting to proceed
Lift	To instruct a helicopter to become airborne and enter the hover
Taxi	This instruction leaves the helicopter pilot free to decide whether to ground taxi or air taxi
Touch Down	This instruction allows the helicopter pilot free to enter a low hover, or touch down on the surface, as appropriate

Figure C7.17
UK helicopter-specific phraseology.

The phrases 'direct departure' and 'direct arrival' are used to indicate that the helicopter can route from or to a specified point on the airfield without following the established visual circuit pattern.

Danger Areas: Certain UK danger areas have a **Danger Area Activity Information Service (DAAIS)** or a **Danger Area Crossing Service (DACS)**.

A DACS service will, when the Danger Area activity permits, provide a clearance for an aircraft to cross the Danger Area under a suitable type of air traffic service. Any crossing clearance provided by a DACS unit is only in relation to the Danger Area activity. The provision of advice and/or traffic information, either inside or operating close to the DA, will be in accordance with the scope of the specific Air Traffic Service provided, ie Deconfliction Service, Traffic Service or Basic Service. When used by a DACS Unit, the term 'active' means that the DA is notified as active and there is activity taking place. Where there is no possibility of confusion, the designation of the Danger Area may be replaced by the name, for example 'Danger Area Loudwater'.

Figure C7.18
A UK Danger Area (D307) as depicted on a UK VFR aeronautical chart.

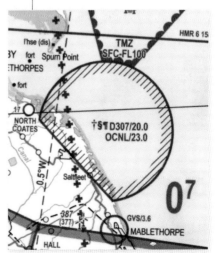

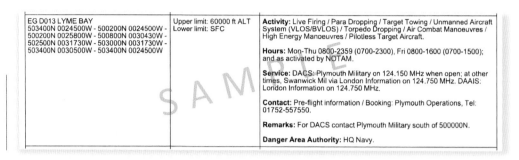

EG D013 LYME BAY 503400N 0024500W - 500200N 0024500W - 500200N 0025800W - 500800N 0030430W - 502500N 0031730W - 503000N 0031730W - 503400N 0030500W - 503400N 0024500W	Upper limit: 60000 ft ALT Lower limit: SFC	**Activity:** Live Firing / Para Dropping / Target Towing / Unmanned Aircraft System (VLOS/BVLOS) / Torpedo Dropping / Air Combat Manoeuvres / High Energy Manoeuvres / Pilotless Target Aircraft.
		Hours: Mon-Thu 0800-2359 (0700-2300), Fri 0800-1600 (0700-1500); and as activated by NOTAM.
		Service: DACS: Plymouth Military on 124.150 MHz when open; at other times, Swanwick Mil via London Information on 124.750 MHz. DAAIS: London Information on 124.750 MHz.
		Contact: Pre-flight information / Booking: Plymouth Operations, Tel: 01752-557550.
		Remarks: For DACS contact Plymouth Military south of 500000N.
		Danger Area Authority: HQ Navy.

Figure C7.19

Details of a Danger Area in the UK AIP, with associated Danger Area Crossing Service (DACS) and Danger Area Activity Information Service (DAAIS).

To obtain a DACS, pilots should call the appropriate unit on the frequency notified in the ENR section of the AIP (where call sign and hours of activity and service will also be found). Where possible, the pilot should provide the DACS unit with an estimated crossing time for the Danger Area:

 "Plymouth Military, G-INDA, request **Crossing Service for Danger Area 007A** *between 1130 and 1200"*

*"G-INDA, Plymouth Military, **Danger Area 007A active, remain outside**".*

Where a crossing is permitted, the following example shows the expected phraseology:

 "Donna Nook Range, Westfly17, **request crossing service for Donna Nook danger area** *between 1530 and 1615".*

*"Westfly17, Donna Nook Range, **Donna Nook danger area crossing approved** between 1530 and 1615, report vacating".*

 "Westfly17, Donna Nook **danger area crossing approved** *between 1530 and 1615, wilco"*

A DAAIS enables pilots to obtain an airborne update of the activity status of a Danger Area, this update will assist the pilot in deciding whether it would be safe to cross the danger area. Information obtained from a DAAIS only relates to the activity status of a Danger Area, information from a DAAIS is not a clearance to cross that Danger Area, whether or not it is active. DAAIS is not a substitute for obtaining as much information as possible on a Danger Area, as part of normal pre-flight briefing procedures.

A typical radio exchange with a DAAIS could take the following form:

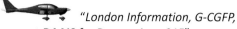 *"London Information, G-CGFP,*
request DAAIS *for Danger Area 215".*

*"G-CGFP, London Information, **Danger Area
215 is not active**".*

It is worth noting that a military controller may refer to an active Danger Area as *"Hot"*, and an inactive danger area as *"Cold"*; but if in doubt, the pilot should always request clarification:

If in doubt, shout

AIRPROX: An **AIRPROX** report should be made by any pilot flying in the UK Flight Information Region, (FIR) if, in the pilot's opinion, the distance between aircraft as well as their relative positions and speed have been such that the safety of the aircraft involved was, or may have been, compromised.

An AIRPROX report should commence with the word *"Airprox"*. If workload is high, the controller may request that a report is filed after landing. If a full report can be made by radio, it takes the following format (although it has to be said, this suggested list seems largely impracticable for a radio report):

- Aircraft call sign
- SSR (transponder) code
- Position of AIRPROX
- Aircraft heading
- Flight level, altitude or height
- Altimeter setting
- Aircraft attitude (level/climbing/descending/turning)
- Weather conditions
- Date and time (UTC) of the AIRPROX
- Description of other aircraft
- First sighting distance and details of flight paths of reporting and reported aircraft.

Perhaps more practically, a written airprox report is to be filed within seven days of the incident, full details can be found in the UK AIP (and there is also an app produced for this purpose by the UK Airprox Board).

Transponder operating procedures

A number of airfields in the UK with responsibility for controlled airspace operate a service called **Frequency Monitoring Codes** – also known to many pilots as 'Listening Squawks'. Pilots operating close to certain areas of controlled airspace and monitoring the relevant frequency (but not requiring an Air Traffic Service) can select the appropriate frequency monitoring code on the transponder (with Altitude mode if available) to indicate that they are monitoring the published ATC frequency. There is no need to establish contact on the frequency, but any pilot using a Frequency Monitoring Code is expected to listen-out on the appropriate frequency for as long as they are squawking the specified transponder code. This facility can also be used by aircraft routing close to certain airfields outside controlled airspace, to notify ATC that the pilot is monitoring their frequency.

Figure C7.20

Details of 'Frequency Monitoring Codes' (listening squawks) in the UK AIP.

2.2.5.6	**Codes in Use**
2.2.5.6.1	* **0010** - This code may be used when flying in the vicinity of the Birmingham Control Zone/Area when the pilot is monitoring Birmingham Radar frequencies.
2.2.5.6.2	* **0011** - This code may be used when flying in the vicinity of Bournemouth Control Zone and monitoring Bournemouth Radar Frequency west of a line between Stoney Cross VRP and Hurst Castle VRP.
2.2.5.6.3	* **0012** - This code may be used when flying outside of London City Controlled Airspace and monitoring Thames Radar Frequency north of a line between Guildford and M20 Junction 2.
2.2.5.6.4	* **0013** - This code may be used when flying outside of Luton Controlled Airspace and monitoring Luton Radar Frequency.
2.2.5.6.5	* **0440** - This code may be used when flying in the vicinity of Edinburgh Control Zones/Areas and monitoring the Edinburgh Approach Frequency 121.200 MHz.
← 2.2.5.6.6	* **2620** - This code may be used when flying within 40 NM of Glasgow Airport and monitoring the Glasgow Approach Frequency 119.100 MHz.

The use of a frequency monitoring code will allow the appropriate Air Traffic Control Unit to attempt to establish contact with an aircraft to prevent an airspace infringement or to resolve potential conflictions. Use of a frequency monitoring codes does not mean that any form of Air Traffic Service is being provided, and the use of such codes does not prevent a pilot from requesting an Air Traffic Service at any time.

An ATC unit attempting to contact an aircraft squawking a frequency monitoring code will make blind transmissions on the appropriate frequency including the transponder code, position, level (if appropriate) and direction of flight of the observed contact. The Mode S-derived call sign/aircraft identification may also be used. A pilot monitoring the frequency who suspects, on the basis of the information provided, that theirs is the aircraft being referred to should respond to Air Traffic Control accordingly. At this point a discrete code may be assigned to confirm identity. Exceptionally, Air Traffic Control may issue immediate instructions or advice to resolve a particular situation. For aircraft outside controlled airspace, Air Traffic Control may request the pilot's compliance with instructions to achieve coordination.

When using a Frequency Monitoring Code, pilots remain responsible for their own separation from other traffic, for navigation and in particular for obtaining permission prior to entering controlled airspace and Aerodrome Traffic Zones (ATZ).

Full details of Frequency Monitoring Codes are found in the 'ENR' section of the UK AIP.

C6 Distress and Urgency Procedures

An **emergency communications and assistance service** is continuously available in the UK on the emergency frequency of 121.5MHz. The service covers most of the UK above 3000ft, but in many areas reception is good below this altitude. The UK AIP states that in an emergency, pilots who have difficulty in establishing communication on the frequency in use should make use of the emergency service on 121.5MHz.

A call on 121.5MHz over the UK is likely to be answered by the RAF-manned Distress and Diversion ('D and D') unit located at the Swanwick ATC centre. Although it is not normally necessary to address a call on the emergency frequency to any particular location, the 'D and D' unit uses the call sign "*London Centre*" – the Swanwick unit can also be contacted via satellite phone, contact numbers are found in the UK AIP. When an aircraft makes a call on the emergency frequency in the UK, its position may be instantaneously displayed to the emergency controllers using a system called 'auto-triangulation', based on VHF Direction Finding (DF) from a number of locations. Auto-triangulation works over most of central and south east England above 3000ft amsl but down to 2000ft amsl in the vicinity of the London airports. Outside the coverage of the auto-triangulation system, aircraft position can still be determined by DF bearing information on 121.5MHz, but this involves manual plotting of the bearings and may take several minutes. The location of aircraft at low altitude using VHF Direction Finding (VDF) may be severely compromised (because of the effects of high ground) over much of Scotland, Wales and south west England. Alternatively, if an aircraft is fitted with a functioning transponder, it can probably be located almost anywhere in the UK in well under a minute unless it is at a particularly low altitude.

The 'D&D' unit has direct access to many other ATC units and all manner of emergency services and facilities to provide whatever assistance is required for an aircraft with an emergency.

Figure C7.21
The UK 'Distress and Diversion' cell at Swanwick.

Figure C7.22
At major UK airports, the fire services can be contacted directly in the event of an incident.

Many major UK airports can communicate on 121.5MHz, and may also have an additional frequency of 121.6MHZ – call sign "[*airfield name*] *Fire*". The **Fire frequency** can be used to communicate directly with the airport's fire service when fire vehicles on the ground are attending an aircraft with an emergency. There are clearly some circumstances where this direct contact between pilot and fire services could be invaluable, but it is not a frequency that should be used except in an actual emergency. No Air Traffic Service is available on the 'Fire' frequency.

The standard format for an **emergency call** is used in the UK, with one additional item because the UK authorities recommend that the pilot qualifications are added to an emergency message, so that the Air Traffic Services can offer appropriate advice and assistance. The following pilot qualifications are considered relevant:

- Student pilot;
- No Instrument Qualification;
- IMC Rating (or Instrument Rating – Restricted);
- Full Instrument Rating.

Student pilots are requested to prefix an initial emergency call with that information, for example:

"*Pan Pan, Pan Pan, Pan Pan, Student G-CMED......*"

Otherwise, pilot qualifications are included with 'other information' at the end of the emergency message, for example:

"***MAYDAY, MAYDAY, MAYDAY***

N *Leeds approach...*

A *Greyair 11, Beech Kingair...*

N *Lightning strike...*

I *intend immediate diversion to Leeds...*

P *current position 10 miles north of Pole Hill*

A *Flight Level 120, heading 120...*

　　Instrument Rating

five POB."

(POB = Persons On Board)

Within the UK a pilot can simulate an 'Urgency' situation, but not a Distress situation, by using the 121.5MHz frequency and addressing their call to 'London Centre'. Before requesting such practice, the pilot should listen-out on frequency for at least a few minutes to ensure that no actual or practice emergency is already in progress. The initial call requesting the practice must make clear that this is a simulated emergency, for example:

 "***Practice Pan, Practice Pan, Practice Pan***, London Centre G-MPLA"

"*G-MPLA, London Centre, **Practice Pan** acknowledged, pass details when ready*"

A pilot can also request a practice position fix on the 121.5MHz frequency – but, if you really are lost, it's much better to say so at the beginning rather than pretending all is well and not receiving the proper priority. When requesting a practice position fix, again it is important to listen-out first to make sure no actual emergency is in progress, a practice position fix can then be requested using the term 'training fix', for example:

 *"Training Fix, Training Fix, Training Fix, London Centre, G-INDY"*

"G-INDY, London Centre, your position is indicated as seven miles east of Lincoln."

Radio operator

A radio in a UK-registered aircraft can only be operated by a person licenced or permitted to use the radio. Student pilots are permitted to operate the radio without a licence, as well as pilots of a balloon or glider who do not communicate by radio with any air traffic control unit, flight information unit or air/ground communications service unit. Other pilots must hold a **Flight Radiotelephony Operator's Licence** (**FRTOL**) to operate the radio in a UK-registered aircraft. To obtain an FRTOL, the applicant must:

- pass the PPL Communications theoretical exam (or equivalent professional exam);

- pass a practical radio Communications test;

- demonstrate English language proficiency to at least level 4.

XII	Flight Radiotelephony Operator's privileges: The holder of this licence has demonstrated competence to operate R/T equipment on board aircraft in English.
XIII	Remarks:

Figure C7.23

Flight Radio Telephony Operator Licence (FRTOL) privileges in an EASA pilot's licence.

Progress check

52. Where will the specific area of Designated Operational Coverage (DOC) be found for a UK communications ATC frequency?
53. What maximum distance from/height above airfield do the CAA recommend as a limit when using the 'Safetycom' frequency?
54. In the UK, how is Flight Level 100 transmitted by radio?
55. What call sign prefix must be used in the UK by a student pilot who do not yet hold a licence and who is flying solo as part of his/her training?
56. In the UK, what is the meaning of the phrase 'Contact'?
57. In the UK, what is the meaning of the phrase 'Hold Short'?
58. What should a pilot expect to receive from an ATSU when operating under a Basic Service?
59. What should a pilot expect to receive from an ATSU when operating under a Traffic Service?
60. When operating under a Traffic Service, who is responsible for terrain clearance?
61. What type of ATC service is a VFR flight most likely to receive when operating inside controlled airspace?
62. When operating under a Radar Control Service, what are the separation minima applied to VFR flights?
63. What call sign suffix is used by a unit providing an aerodrome Air/Ground Communication Service (AGCS)?
64. In the UK Standard Overhead Join, in what location does the aircraft descend to circuit height/altitude?
65. Under what circumstances can an aircraft in the UK 'land after' another aircraft already occupying the runway?
66. Under what circumstances can a UK Aerodrome Flight Information Service Officer (AFISO) issue instructions?
67. Under what circumstances should the 'Safetycom' frequency be used?
68. What is the recommended minimum distance/flying time at which to establish contact with an ATSU when planning to cross a MATZ?
69. What is the correct 'Q' code for a VDF bearing from the aircraft to the station, accurate to within +/- 5°?
70. In the UK, what action must a pilot take before entering an RMZ?
71. How is a helicopter expected to proceed if cleared to 'Air-Taxi'?
72. In relation to a Danger Area, what is a DAAIS?
73. How should a Frequency Monitoring Code ('Listening Squawk') be used by a pilot?
74. In the UK, which pilots are required to hold a Flight Radiotelephony Operator's Licence (FRTOL)?

These questions are intended to test knowledge and reinforce some of the key learning points from this section. In answering these questions, a 'pass rate' of about 80% should be the target.

Model answers are found at page C95

COM Progress Test Answers

C1 VHF Radio Broadcast

1. The Very High Frequency (VHF) band, specifically between 118MHz and 137MHz.
2. That VHF radio waves travel in a straight line and so range is determined by the 'line of sight' principle.
3. As the aircraft height increases, the range of its VHF radio transmissions will also increase.
4. In conditions such as 'duct propagation or 'sporadic E'.

C2 Transmission Technique

5. Romeo, **ROW** ME OH.
6. **FOW**-er.
7. Each digit should be transmitted separately, particularly in the case of call signs, headings, runways, wind direction and speed.
8. Any of: aircraft level, cloud base, visibility, a transponder code of whole thousands.
9. One Two Zero Decimal Four Zero Five.
10. One Three Six Decimal Seven.
11. 15:30.
12. G-WR.
13. An ATC clearance is an authorisation for an aircraft to proceed under the conditions specified.
14. A service provided to give advice and information useful for the safe and efficient conduct of flights.
15. An ATSU providing neither an ATC nor Flight Information Service.
16. In the Aeronautical Information Publication (AIP), or commercially available flight guides.

C3 VFR Communications Procedures

17. The radio transmission is readable, but with difficulty.
18. Distress call and messages.
19. Repeat all, or a specified part, of this message exactly as you received it.
20. I have received all of your last transmission.
21. Understood, will comply.
22. '[callsign] ready for departure'.
23. This is a conditional clearance.
24. Descend to and maintain [level].
25. The aircraft is lined up with the landing runway, at a distance of between 4nm and 8nm from the runway.
26. An Aerodrome Flight Information Service – an ATSU providing information and advice at a specific airfield.

27. Choose any five from the following list:
    * Altimeter Settings (including units when value is below 1000 hectopascals)
    * Runway in Use
    * Airways or Route Clearances
    * SSR (transponder) Instructions
    * Taxi/Towing Instructions
    * Clearance to Enter, Land On, Take-Off On, Backtrack, Cross, or Hold Short of any active runway
    * Level Instructions
    * Heading Instructions
    * Speed Instructions
    * Frequency Changes
    * Type of Air Traffic Service
    * Transition Levels
    * Approach Clearances
    * VDF Information
28. Establish communications with [call sign][frequency].
29. 'Wait and I will call you', no clearance or permission is granted with this phrase.
30. It should be operated at all times in-flight, unless an ATC unit requires otherwise.
31. Operate the 'ident' function of the transponder.
32. My transponder is set to [code] [mode].
33. The aircraft's pressure altitude is transmitted.
34. 7000
35. 7700
36. 11 o'clock.

C4 Weather Information

37. An Automatic Terminal Information Service – an automated broadcast of information for a specific airfield including the current weather, runway in use, and any specific procedures, navigational warnings and/or equipment unserviceability's.
38. In the relevant Aeronautical Information Publication (AIP).
39. VOLMET

C5 Communications Failure

40. A blind transmission is a transmission from one station to another where two-way communication cannot be established, but where it is believed that the station being called is able to receive the transmission.
41. • • • • (four very short transmissions).
42. A steady green light
43. Move clear of the landing area.
44. Rocking the aircraft's wings.
45. Say Again.

C6 Distress and Urgency Procedures

46. 121.5MHz.
47. A condition of being threatened by serious and/or imminent danger and requiring immediate assistance.
48. *"Mayday, Mayday, Mayday; Haworth approach this is AeroAir2, Cessna 182, engine failure. Intend forced landing, current position two miles south of Hightown, altitude 3000 feet heading 180°, three Persons On Board."*
49. An urgency situation, spoken words 'Pan Pan'.
50. *"Pan Pan, Pan Pan, Pan Pan; Northly Information this is G-BREW, PA-28, rough running engine, routing directly to overhead the airfield. Three miles east of the airfield, altitude 2000 feet, heading 270°, one Person On Board."*
51. Urgency calls take priority over all other radio messages except distress messages.

C7 National Procedures

52. In the UK Aeronautical Information Publication (AIP).
53. No more than 10nm from the airfield and no higher than 2000ft above the airfield, or not more than 1000ft above the published circuit height/altitude.
54. Flight Level Wun Hundred.
55. 'Student'
56. Establish communications with [ATSU] – your details have been passed to them.
57. Stop before reaching the specified location.
58. Advice and information which may include weather information, changes of serviceability of facilities, conditions at aerodromes, general airspace activity information, and any other information likely to affect safety. Avoiding other traffic is solely the pilot's responsibility. Pilots should not expect any form of traffic information from a controller/FISO when operating under a Basic Service and the pilot remains responsible for collision avoidance at all times.
59. In addition to the provisions of a Basic Service, the controller provides specific surveillance-derived traffic information to assist the pilot in avoiding other traffic. Nevertheless, ultimately the avoidance of other traffic is solely the pilot's responsibility.
60. The pilot remains responsible for terrain clearance at all times.
61. A Radar Control Service.
62. If traffic avoidance advice is issued to a VFR or Special VFR flight under a Radar Control Service, the controller is not required to maintain any specific minimum distance between a VFR/SVFR flight and other traffic. The pilot of a VFR or Special VFR flight is ultimately responsible for maintaining a safe separation from other traffic.
63. 'Radio'
64. On the 'deadside' of the circuit.

65. In the UK aircraft must not land on a runway if there is already another aircraft on the runway, unless an air traffic control unit at the airfield authorises an aircraft to land after. When an ATC unit chooses to permit a 'land after' the following restrictions apply:
    - The runway must be long enough to complete the 'land after' safely;
    - The landings must take place during daylight hours;
    - The second landing aircraft must be able to see the first aircraft clearly and continuously until it is clear of the runway;
    - The second landing aircraft must have been warned.

66. A UK AFISO can issue instructions and information to aircraft on the apron and manoeuvring area to assist pilots in preventing collisions between aircraft and vehicles/obstructions on the manoeuvring area, or between aircraft moving on the apron. A UK AFISO can also issue instructions to vehicles and persons on the manoeuvring area.

67. Only at airfields which do not have a notified radio frequency. If an airfield has a notified frequency, that should be used even outside the notified operating hours.

68. Not less than 15nm distance or 5 minutes flying time from the MATZ.

69. QDM, class B.

70. Before entering a UK Radio Mandatory Zone (RMZ), the pilot must make an initial call to the unit controlling the RMZ, and this call must be acknowledged by ATC. The phrase 'standby' does not constitute acknowledgement of an initial call.

71. Used in place of 'taxi', the helicopter is expected to proceed at a slow speed above the surface, normally below 20 knots and in ground effect.

72. A DAAIS (Danger Area Activity Information Service) enables pilots to obtain an airborne update of the activity status of a Danger Area, this update will assist the pilot in deciding whether it would be safe to cross the danger area. Information obtained from a DAAIS only relates to the activity status of a Danger Area, information from a DAAIS is not a clearance to cross that Danger Area, whether or not it is active.

73. Pilots operating close to certain areas of controlled airspace and monitoring the relevant frequency (but not requiring an Air Traffic Service) can select the appropriate frequency monitoring code on the transponder (with Altitude mode if available) to indicate that they are monitoring the published ATC frequency.

74. A radio in a UK-registered aircraft can only be operated by a person licenced or permitted to use the radio. Student pilots are permitted to operate the radio without a licence, as well as pilots of a balloon or glider who do not communicate by radio with any air traffic control unit, flight information unit or air/ground communications service unit.

Appendix 1 Sample radio conversations, UK procedures

A VFR departure from a controlled airfield

"Broughton Ground, Fastnet 15 on the south apron, information B, request taxi"

"Fastnet 15, Broughton Ground, taxi via taxiway D to holding point D1, runway 32, QNH 1007"

"Taxi via taxiway D to holding point D1, runway 32, QNH 1007, Fastnet 15"

"Fastnet 15, holding point D1, ready for departure"

"Fastnet 15, roger, hold position. Your clearance is to depart VFR to leave the zone via Oldtown VRP, not above 2,500ft QNH 1007"

"Holding. Cleared to depart to leave the zone via Oldtown VRP, VFR, not above 2,500ft, 1007, Fastnet 15"

"Fastnet 15, read-back correct, hold position and contact Broughton Tower 118.975"

"Hold position, contact Broughton Tower 118.975, Fastnet 15"

"Broughton Tower, Fastnet 15, holding at holding point D1"

"Fastnet 15, Broughton Tower, are you ready for immediate departure?"

"Affirm, Fastnet 15"

"Fastnet 15, runway 32 cleared immediate take-off, surface wind 300 degrees 10 knots"

"Runway 32 cleared immediate take-off, Fastnet 15"

Once the aircraft is airborne and has climbed to a reasonable height

"Fastnet 15, report passing Oldtown"

"Wilco Fastnet 15"

"Fastnet 15 passing Oldtown"

"Fastnet 15, roger, the Bardy 1004, suggest you freecall Lindley Zone 125.6"

"Bardy QNH 1004, will freecall Lindley Zone 125.6, Fastnet 15"

A VFR departure from an airfield with an Aerodrome Flight Information Service (AFIS)

"Middleton Information, EI-SAC request airfield information and taxi instructions"

"E-AC, Runway in use 25, QNH 997 hectopascals, taxi holding point A for Runway 25 via the Southern taxiway"

"Runway 25, QNH 997 hectopascals, taxi holding point A via the Southern taxiway, E-AC"

"Ready for departure, E-AC"

"E-AC, traffic is a Cessna 172 left-hand late downwind, report lined up runway 25"

"Traffic in sight, wilco E-AC"

"E-AC lined-up runway 25"

"E-AC, roger, traffic is now left base. Surface wind 230 degrees seven knots. Runway 25 take-off at your discretion"

"Runway 25 taking-off, E-AC"

Once the aircraft is airborne and has climbed to a reasonable height

"E-AC, no reported traffic to the west, report when leaving the frequency"

"Wilco, E-AC"

A VFR departure from an airfield with an Air Ground Communication Service (AGCS)

"Elmdon Radio, G-GGJK request airfield information for local VFR flight"

"G-JK, Elmdon Radio, runway in use 19 Left, surface wind 200 degrees 12 knots, QNH 1025"

"Taxiing for Runway 19 Left, QNH 1025, G-JK"

"G-JK, ready for departure"

"G-JK, traffic is a DA40 at one mile final"

"Traffic in sight, holding position, G-JK"

"G-JK, ready for departure"

"G-JK, no reported traffic, surface wind is 210 degrees, 10 knots"

"Roger, taking-off, G-JK"

An initial en-route call

 "Donington Radar, F-GNZF"

 "F-GNZF, Donington Radar, pass your message"

 "F-GNZF is a Jodel from Westham to Eastley, overhead Carley at 3,000 feet QNH 1014, VFR, squawking 7000, request traffic service"

 "F-ZF, roger, squawk 4054"

 "Squawk 4054, F-ZF"

 "F-ZF identified 1 mile north of Carley, traffic service"

 *"Traffic service, F-ZF"*

 "F-ZF, limited traffic information from the right for the next five miles due to limits of surveillance cover"

 "Roger, F-ZF"

 "F-ZF, traffic 11 o'clock three miles crossing left to right, no height information"

 "Traffic in sight, F-ZF"

A VFR Flight Crossing Controlled Airspace

 "Hayes Zone, G-IZOB"

 "G-IZOB, Hayes Zone, pass your message"

 "G-IZOB is a Colibri routing from a private site near Carlton to Warley airfield, two miles east of Detham at 1,500 feet QNH 1011, VFR, request zone transit"

"G-OB, Roger, remain clear of controlled airspace, squawk 6530"

 "Wilco, squawk 6530 G-OB"

"G-OB, identified, cleared to enter controlled airspace on current track, not above 1,500 feet Haynes QNH 1013, VFR, report at Overton VRP"

 "Cleared to enter controlled airspace on current track, not above 1,500 feet Haynes QNH 1013, wilco, G-OB"

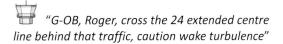 *"Overhead Overton, G-OB"*

"G-OB, Roger, radar control service, traffic 12 o-clock five miles is an A320 on three mile final for runway 24"

 "Traffic in sight, G-OB"

 "G-OB, Roger, cross the 24 extended centre line behind that traffic, caution wake turbulence"

 "Cross behind the A320, roger, G-OB"

"G-OB, clear of controlled airspace, basic service"

"Basic service, G-OB"

Arrival at a Controlled Airfield

 "Lancester Approach, Silmed 14"

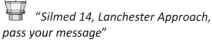 *"Silmed 14, Lanchester Approach, pass your message"*

 "Silmed 14 is a PA28 inbound from Stoneham, overhead Wantly 2000 feet 1016, VFR, estimate zone boundary in five minutes, we have Information Delta"

"Silmed 14, roger, Information Delta is current, squawk 4025 and report at Theale"

 "Squawk 4025, wilco, Silmed 14"

 "Silmed 14 overhead Theale"

"Silmed 14, cleared to enter controlled airspace VFR, routing directly to the airfield not above 2500 feet, 1016. Report airfield in sight"

 "Cleared to enter controlled airspace routing to the airfield, VFR, not above 2500 feet, 1016, wilco, Silmed 14"

 "Airfield in sight, Silmed 14"

"Silmed 14, continue towards left base for Runway 25, contact Lancester Tower 118.475"

 "Continue towards left base for Runway 25, contact Lanchester Tower 118.475, Silmed 14"

 "Lancester Tower, Silmed 14"

"Silmed 14 Lancester Tower, cleared to final, number one"

"Cleared to final number one, Silmed 14"

"Final Runway 25, Silmed 14"

"Silmed 14, surface wind 230 degrees seven knots, Runway 25 cleared to land"

"Runway 25, cleared to land, Silmed 14"

"Silmed 14 vacate right on taxiway Delta, contact Ground 121.7"

 "Vacate right on taxiway Delta, contact Ground 121.7, Silmed 14"

 "Lanchester Ground, Silmed 14"

"Silmed 14 continue on taxiway Delta to the GA apron"

"Taxiway Delta to the GA apron, Silmed 14"

Note: The pilot may include the runway designator in 'downwind' and 'final' position reports if there is the potential for confusion.

Arrival at an AFIS airfield

 "Hardy Information, G-DAVE"

 *"G-DAVE, Hardy Information, pass your message"*

"G-DAVE is a Jodel inbound from Madding, five miles south of the airfield, VFR, 1900 feet 1006, request airfield information"

"G-VE, runway in use is 16, left-hand circuit, QNH 1006, QFE 1001, traffic is a PA38 in the circuit, currently left-hand downwind, report overhead for overhead join"

"Runway 16, QNH1006, QFE 1001, looking for traffic, wilco, G-VE"

"G-VE overhead, descending deadside"

"G-VE, roger. Traffic is left base Runway 16"

"Traffic in sight, G-VE"

"Downwind, G-VE"

"G-VE, roger, report final"

"Wilco G-VE"

"G-VE, final Runway 16"

"G-VE, surface wind 180 degrees 10 knots. Runway 16 land at your discretion"

"Landing 16, G-VE"

"G-VE, landing traffic one mile final, vacate next right"

"Vacate next right, G-VE"

"G-VE, continue to the flying school via the parallel taxiway"

"To the flying school via the parallel taxiway, G-VE"

Note: The pilot may include the runway designator in 'downwind' and 'final' position reports if there is the potential for confusion.

Arrival at AGCS airfield

 "Stretford Radio, G-HYLB"

 "G-HYLB, Stretford radio, pass your message"

 "G-HYLB, Slingsby six miles east of the airfield, 3000 feet 998 hectopascals, VFR, inbound for landing request joining information"

 "G-LB, Stretford radio, runway in use 09 left hand, QNH 998 hectopascals, QFE 994 hectopascals, one aircraft about to depart to the east"

 "Runway 09 left hand, QNH 998 hectopascals, QFE 994 hectopascals, G-LB"

 "G-LB, joining overhead for Runway 09"

 "G-LB, roger, previously reported traffic lining up Runway 09"

 "G-LB, downwind Runway 09"

 "G-LB, roger"

 "G-LB, final Runway 09"

 "G-LB, roger, surface wind 120 degrees 15 knots"

 "Roger, G-LB"

 "G-LB backtracking Runway 09 to vacate at Bravo"

"G-LB, roger, no reported traffic"

Note: The pilot may include the runway designator in 'downwind' and 'final' position reports if there is the potential for confusion.

Visual circuits at a controlled airfield

"Mallory Tower, Signet 03, Information Bravo, request taxi"

"Signet 03, runway in use 22 left hand, QNH 1002. Give way to the DA40 crossing ahead of you left to right then taxi holding point A, hold short of runway 15"

"Runway 22, QNH 1002, after the DA40 taxi holding point A, hold short Runway 15"

"Holding short Runway 15, Signet 03"

"Signet 03, hold position, departing traffic Runway 15"

"Hold position, Signet 03"

"Signet 03, cross Runway 15 to holding point A, report ready for departure"

"Cross Runway 15 to holding point A, wilco, Signet 03"

"Signet 03, ready for departure"

"Signet 03, behind the landing Duchess, line-up Runway 22, behind"

"Behind the landing Duchess, line-up Runway 22, behind, Signet 03"

"Signet 03, surface wind 220 degrees five knots. Runway 22 cleared take-off"

"Runway 22 cleared take-off, Signet 03"

"Signet 03 downwind for touch and go"

"Signet 03, you are number two, traffic is a Cessna 172 on base leg"

"Number two, traffic in sight, Signet 03"

"Signet 03 final, touch and go"

"Signet 03, continue approach"

"Continue approach, Signet 03"

"Signet 03, surface wind 210 degrees seven knots. Runway 22 cleared touch and go"

"Cleared touch and go, Signet 03"

"Signet 03 downwind for flapless approach"

"Signet 03, report before turning base, traffic about to depart"

"Wilco, Signet 03"

"Signet 03, ready to turn base"

"Signet 03, orbit left"

"Orbit left, Signet 03"

"Signet 03, continue to final number 1"

"Number one continue to final, Signet 03"

"Signet 03 final, touch and go"

"Signet 03, surface wind 210 degrees five knots. Runway 22 cleared touch and go"

"Runway 22 cleared touch and go, Signet 03"

"Signet 03, Fanstop"

"Report climbing away, Signet 03"

"Climbing away, Signet 03"

"Signet 03 roger, report downwind"

"Wilco, Signet 03"

"Signet 03, downwind, glide approach"

"Signet 03 roger, report final"

"Wilco, Signet 03"

"Signet 03, final Runway 22"

"Signet 03, surface wind 220 degrees eight knots. Runway 22 cleared touch and go"

"Runway 22 cleared touch and go, Signet 03"

"Signet 03, go-around, I say again go-around, vehicle on runway"

"Going around, Signet 03"

"Signet 03, climb straight ahead to 1000 feet before turning crosswind"

"Climb straight ahead to 1000 feet, Signet 03"

"Signet 03, downwind to land"

"Signet 03, No 2 to an Airbus 320 on three mile final, caution wake turbulence"

"No 2, traffic in sight, Signet 03"

"Signet 03, final Runway 22 to land"

"Signet 03, surface wind 220 degrees four knot. Runway 22, land after the Airbus, caution wake turbulence"

"Runway 22 land after, Signet 03"

"Signet 03, vacate left at Charlie, expedite, landing traffic two miles"

"Vacate left at Charlie, Signet 03"

"Signet 03, cleared to taxi to the flying school apron. Cleared to cross runway 15"

"Taxi to the flying school apron, cleared to cross runway 15, Signet 03"

Appendix 2 Standard Phraseology

Word/Phrase	Meaning	Notes
ACKNOWLEDGE	Let me know that you have received and understood this message	
AFFIRM	Yes	
APPROVED	Permission for the proposed action is granted	
BLOCK	Indicates an aircraft wishes to operate within a vertical block of airspace, the lower and upper limits are usually defined as flight levels	UK military phraseology
BREAK	Notifies a separation between different portions of a message	Can be used where there is no clear distinction between different parts of the message
BREAK BREAK	Indicates the separation between messages to different aircraft	
CANCEL	Annul the previously transmitted clearance	
CHANGING TO	I intend to call [unit] on [frequency]	UK phraseology
CHECK	Examine a system or procedure	No response is normally expected to this instruction
CHECK ALTIMETER SETTING AND CONFIRM [LEVEL]	Check the selected pressure setting and confirm your current level	
CLEARED	Authorised to proceed under the conditions specified	
CONFIRM	I request verification of a clearance, instruction, action or information	
CONFIRM [LEVEL]	Check and report your current level	
CONFIRM SQUAWK	Confirm the code / mode selected on the transponder	The pilot is expected to: – Check the code setting on the transponder; – Reselect the code if necessary; and – Confirm to ATC the code and mode selected on the transponder
CONTACT	Establish communications with [call sign] [frequency]….	
CONTACT	Establish communications with [ATSU] – your details have been passed to them	UK phraseology, this is slightly different to the ICAO/EASA definition of this word
CONTACT	A radar handover to the next controller has taken place	UK military phraseology
CONTINUE WITH	Used when it is known that an aircraft has already established contact with another unit, or when details have been passed to the next unit but no radar handover has taken place	UK phraseology
CONTINUE WITH	Your details are known to the next controller, but no radar hand over has taken place	UK military phraseology
CORRECT	True or accurate	
CORRECTION	An error has been made in this transmission (or the message indicated). The correct version is….	UK phraseology
DISREGARD	Ignore	

Word/Phrase	Meaning	Notes
FANSTOP	I am initiating a practice engine failure after take-off	UK phraseology. Used only by pilots of single engine aircraft. The response from the ATSU should be *"Report climbing away"*.
FREECALL	Call [ATSU] – your details have not been passed to them	UK phraseology. Used mostly by military units
HOLD SHORT	Stop before reaching the specified location	UK phraseology. Only used in limited circumstances where no defined point exists, or to emphasis a clearance limit
HOW DO YOU READ?	What is the readability of my transmission?	
I SAY AGAIN	I repeat for emphasis or clarity	
MAINTAIN	Continue in accordance with the conditions specified	Can also be used in the literal sense – eg *"Maintain VFR"*
MONITOR	Listen out on [call sign] [frequency]....	
NEGATIVE	No, or Permission is not granted, or That is not correct, or Not capable	
OUT	This exchange of transmissions is ended and I **do not** expect a response	Rarely used in normal communications
OVER	My transmissions is over and I **do** expect a response	Rarely used in normal communications
READ BACK	Repeat all, or a specified part, of this message exactly as received	
RECLEARED	A change has been made to your last clearance, this new clearance supersedes your previous clearance or part of it	
REPORT	Pass me the following information	
REQUEST	I would like to know, or I want to obtain	
RESET SQUAWK [CODE]	Reselect the assigned transponder code	
ROGER	I have received all of your last transmission	This only means the message has been received, it does not mean the message will be acted upon and must not be used in place of Affirm or Negative.
SAY AGAIN	Repeat all, or a specified part, of you last transmission	
SPEAK SLOWER	Reduce your rate of speech	
SQUAWK [CODE] [MODE]	Set the specified transponder code as instructed.	Unless instructed otherwise, pilots should always select 'Altitude' mode (ALT / Mode C) on, even if ATC do not specify the mode
SQUAWK ALTITUDE	Select the 'Altitude /Mode C' function on the transponder	
SQUAWK CHARLIE	Select the 'Altitude /Mode C' function on the transponder	

Word/Phrase	Meaning	Notes
SQUAWK EMERGENCY or SQUAWK 7700	UK phraseology. Select the emergency transponder code (7700)	
SQUAWK IDENT	Operate the 'Ident' function on the transponder	
SQUAWK MAYDAY	Select the Emergency transponder code	This code is 7700
SQUAWK STANDBY	Set the transponder to 'standby' mode	In this mode the transponder does not transmit
SQUAWKING [CODE] [MODE]	My transponder is set to [code] [mode]	
STANDBY	Wait and I will call you	No response is expected and no form of clearance or permission is granted (or denied) by this phrase
STOP SQUAWK	Set the transponder to standby or off so that it is not transmitting	
STOP SQUAWK ALTITUDE	Deselect the altitude reporting function of the transponder	
STOP SQUAWK ALTITUDE – WRONG INDICATION	Deselect the altitude reporting function of the transponder, the level readout is incorrect	
STOP SQUAWK CHARLIE	Deselect the altitude reporting function of the transponder	
STOP SQUAWK CHARLIE – WRONG INDICATION	Deselect the altitude reporting function of the transponder, the level readout is incorrect	
UNABLE	I cannot comply with your request, instruction or clearance	When this word is used, a reason should normally be given
WILCO	Understood, will comply	Abbreviated from "**Will Co**mply", should not be used where a 'read back' is required (as described shortly).
WORDS TWICE	(As a request): Communication is difficult, transmit every word, or group of words, twice (As information): Because communications are difficult, every word, or group of words, in this message will be transmitted twice	

Index

C117